1st EDITION

Perspectives on Diseases and Disorders

Post-Traumatic Stress Disorder

Carrie Fredericks
Book Editor

Detroit • New York • San Francisco • New Haven, Conn • Waterville, Maine • London

Christine Nasso, *Publisher*
Elizabeth Des Chenes, *Managing Editor*

© 2010 Greenhaven Press, a part of Gale, Cengage Learning

Articles in Greenhaven Press anthologies are often edited for length to meet page requirements. In addition, original titles of these works are changed to clearly present the main thesis and to explicitly indicate the author's opinion. Every effort is made to ensure that Greenhaven Press accurately reflects the original intent of the authors. Every effort has been made to trace the owners of copyrighted material.

Cover image © Radius Images/Alamy

LIBRARY OF CONGRESS CATALOGING-IN-PUBLICATION DATA

Post-traumatic stress disorder / Carrie Fredericks, book editor.
    p. cm. -- (Perspectives on diseases and disorders)
  Includes bibliographical references and index.
  ISBN 978-0-7377-4554-2 (hardcover)
  1. Post-traumatic stress disorder. I. Fredericks, Carrie.
  RC552.P67P6635 2009
  616.85'21--dc22

                                                            2009020984

Printed in the United States of America
 2 3 4 5 6 7 13 12 11 10

CONTENTS

FOREWORD

"Medicine, to produce health, has to examine disease."
—Plutarch

Independent research on a health issue is often the first step to complement discussions with a physician. But locating accurate, well-organized, understandable medical information can be a challenge. A simple Internet search on terms such as "cancer" or "diabetes," for example, returns an intimidating number of results. Sifting through the results can be daunting, particularly when some of the information is inconsistent or even contradictory. The Greenhaven Press series Perspectives on Diseases and Disorders offers a solution to the often overwhelming nature of researching diseases and disorders.

From the clinical to the personal, titles in the Perspectives on Diseases and Disorders series provide students and other researchers with authoritative, accessible information in unique anthologies that include basic information about the disease or disorder, controversial aspects of diagnosis and treatment, and first-person accounts of those impacted by the disease. The result is a well-rounded combination of primary and secondary sources that, together, provide the reader with a better understanding of the disease or disorder.

Each volume in Perspectives on Diseases and Disorders explores a particular disease or disorder in detail. Material for each volume is carefully selected from a wide range of sources, including encyclopedias, journals, newspapers, nonfiction books, speeches, government documents, pamphlets, organization newsletters, and position papers. Articles in the first chapter provide an authoritative, up-to-date overview that covers symptoms, causes and effects, treatments, cures, and medical advances. The second chapter presents a substantial number of opposing viewpoints on controversial treatments and other current debates relating to the volume topic. The third chapter offers a variety of personal perspectives on the disease or disorder. Patients, doctors, caregivers, and loved ones represent just some of the voices found in this narrative chapter.

Each Perspectives on Diseases and Disorders volume also includes:

- An **annotated table of contents** that provides a brief summary of each article in the volume.
- An **introduction** specific to the volume topic.
- Full-color **charts and graphs** to illustrate key points, concepts, and theories.
- Full-color **photos** that show aspects of the disease or disorder and enhance textual material.
- **"Fast Facts"** that highlight pertinent additional statistics and surprising points.
- A **glossary** providing users with definitions of important terms.
- A **chronology** of important dates relating to the disease or disorder.
- An annotated list of **organizations to contact** for students and other readers seeking additional information.
- A **bibliography** of additional books and periodicals for further research.
- A detailed **subject index** that allows readers to quickly find the information they need.

Whether a student researching a disorder, a patient recently diagnosed with a disease, or an individual who simply wants to learn more about a particular disease or disorder, a reader who turns to Perspectives on Diseases and Disorders will find a wealth of information in each volume that offers not only basic information, but also vigorous debate from multiple perspectives.

INTRODUCTION

On April 20, 1999, two male students at Columbine High School in Littleton, Colorado, killed twelve students and one teacher and injured more than twenty others at the school before committing suicide. This shooting shocked the nation, and people began thinking about violence in video games, bullying in schools, and how post-traumatic stress impacts children. Before this shooting, post-traumatic stress disorder (PTSD) had often been considered to be mainly in the realm of war, rape, or natural disasters, but as time passed and students and adults in Littleton sought mental health assistance, it became apparent that many suffered from PTSD.

The post-traumatic stress disorder risk factors for children differ greatly from those of adults. For adults, risk factors include being female, being middle age (forty to sixty), having little experience with traumatic events, belonging to an ethnic minority group, being in a lower socioeconomic group, and having children in the home. For children, the three main risk factors for developing PTSD are the severity of the traumatic event, the reaction of parents to the child and the event, and the closeness of the child to the event.

For children, the severity of a traumatic event is very important in the development of adolescent PTSD. Research has shown that certain types of trauma may lead to higher PTSD incidence. According to the U.S. government's National Center for Posttraumatic Stress Disorder, "Research suggests that interpersonal traumas such as rape and assault are more likely to result in PTSD than other types of traumas. Additionally, if an individual has experienced a number of traumatic events in the past, those experiences increase the risk of developing PTSD."[1]

The reaction of parents is very influential for children who have experienced a traumatic event. The amount of stress that a parent shows in the aftermath of a traumatic event has a large impact on a child. The less stress that parents experience or show to a child the less likely that child will develop stress problems. eMedicine.com, a medical reference site for physicians and health care professionals, reports that "parental reaction is a critical factor affecting the child's reaction. Parents' anxiety and difficulty coping with life as a result of the trauma may overwhelm a child, whereas parental ability to cope and to provide a safe haven for a child may affect the child's ability to deal with the stressor or the propensity to develop protracted PTSD."[2]

The proximity of the child to the traumatic event is the third of the major risk factors. A child who is an eyewitness to an event is much more likely to develop PTSD than one who only finds out about it after the fact. The National Center for Posttraumatic Stress Disorder reports, "Studies have shown that as many as 100% of children who witness a parental homicide or sexual assault develop PTSD. Similarly, 90% of sexually abused children, 77% of children exposed to a school shooting, and 35% of urban youth exposed to community violence develop PTSD."[3] The media also play a roll in adolescent PTSD. When a tragedy occurs it is often replayed in various media outlets, especially when it involves a large number of victims or witnesses. Repeatedly viewing a traumatic event increases the likelihood that a child will develop PTSD symptoms.

The way children react to a traumatic event can be drastically different from the reactions of adults. According to the National Center for Posttraumatic Stress Disorder, children of different ages can also react in different ways. For very young children, not many PTSD

The 1999 Columbine High School shooting tragedy shocked the nation, and people began to think about the effects of post-traumatic stress disorder on children. (Gary Caskey/Reuters/ Landov)

symptoms apply. This may largely be due to the fact that the very young are not able to verbalize what they are thinking and feeling. One of the primary reactions can be the loss or delay of a developmental skill like potty training. School-age children often re-create the event through drawings and while playing alone or with others. Many also think that if they pay very close attention they will be able to tell when something bad is going to happen. For teenagers, the symptoms of PTSD look a lot like those seen in adults. One of the main actions that teenagers may take is to be more verbal and aggressive when experiencing these adultlike symptoms.

Another way children react differently from adults is through a symptom called dissociation. According to the Society for the Study of Trauma and Dissociation, this symptom is one of the hallmarks of post-traumatic stress disorder, and the Sidran Institute, a traumatic stress and education advocacy group, reports that children are much more likely to dissociate memories of a traumatic event than adults are. With this symptom, a child will become more and more detached from what is happening around him or her and also become detached from his or her own feelings and emotions. The Sidran Institute also reports, "Research shows that the younger the child is at the time of the trauma, the less likely the event will be remembered."[4]

When the Columbine shooting occurred, Kacy Ruegsegger was in the school library. She was shot in the right shoulder, through the right hand, and had a graze wound on her neck. She survived by pretending to be dead. She later became a nurse and gave credit to the nurses who took care of her for inspiring her career choice. In April 2007 Ruegsegger, now Ruegsegger Johnson, told CNN that when she realized that she had survived the shooting spree, she was overwhelmed with fear. "I didn't want to be in public. I didn't want anyone knowing my name. I was afraid—from the post-traumatic stress—that somebody was going to finish me off. To normal people that makes no sense, but to a victim of something like that— to me—it made perfect sense."[5] The CNN article also describes her recurring physical and mental issues: "She still has physical scars—she's on disability from her job as a nurse because of recurring pain from her injury. And she has emotional wounds as well—she's susceptible to 'triggers'—sights or sounds that bring back vivid memories of gunfire, of sirens and helicopters."[6] Almost ten years after the Columbine shooting Ruegsegger Johnson has a satisfying life. "I feel normal. It's a different kind of normal, but it's normal."[7]

Notes

1. National Center for Posttraumatic Stress Disorder, "PTSD in Children and Adolescents," U.S. Department of Veterans Affairs, 2008. www.ncptsd.va.gov.

2. eMedicine.com, "Posttraumatic Stress Disorder in Children: Overview," Medscape, 2009. http://emedicine.medscape.com.

3. National Center for Posttraumatic Stress Disorder, "PTSD in Children and Adolescents."

4. Sidran Institute, "What Are Traumatic Memories?" 1994. www.sidran.org.

5. Quoted in Mary Carter, "Columbine Survivor: Expect an Emotional Roller Coaster," CNN, April 20, 2007. www.cnn.com.

6. Mary Carter, "Columbine Survivor: Expect an Emotional Roller Coaster."

7. Quoted in Mary Carter, "Columbine Survivor: Expect an Emotional Roller Coaster."

CHAPTER 1

Understanding PTSD

An Overview of Post-Traumatic Stress Disorder

Jacqueline L. Longe and Ken R. Wells

In the following selection Jacqueline L. Longe and Ken R. Wells provide an overview of post-traumatic stress disorder (PTSD), covering characteristics, risk factors, causes, symptoms, and treatments. Although PTSD has several significant characteristics, say the authors, these vary in severity from patient to patient. The important factors in the treatment of PTSD include medications and therapies, and these treatments are usually individualized for each case. Longe is a medical writer and editor. Wells is a medical writer.

Post-traumatic stress disorder (PTSD) is a debilitating psychological condition triggered by a major traumatic event, such as rape, war, a terrorist act, death of a loved one, a natural disaster, or a catastrophic accident. It is marked by upsetting memories or thoughts of the ordeal, "blunting" of emotions, increased arousal, and sometimes severe personality changes.

SOURCE: Jacqueline L. Longe and Ken R. Wells, "Post-Traumatic Stress Disorder," *The Gale Encyclopedia of Medicine,* 2007. Copyright © 2008 Gale Cengage Learning. Reproduced by permission of Gale, a part of Cengage Learning.

Photo on facing page. PTSD was Initially diagnosed in war veterans, but research has found that PTSD also affects victims of rape and other violent crimes and natural disasters. (**AP Images**)

PTSD: Description and Statistics

Officially termed post-traumatic stress disorder since 1980, PTSD was once known as shell shock or battle fatigue because of its more common manifestation in war veterans. However, in the past 20 years, PTSD has been diagnosed in rape victims and victims of violent crime; survivors of natural disasters; the families of loved ones lost in the downing of Flight 103 over Lockerbie, Scotland; and survivors of the 1993 World Trade Center bombing, the 1995 Oklahoma City bombing, the random school and workplace shootings, and the release of poisonous gas in a Japanese subway; and in the September 11, 2001, World Trade Center and Pentagon terrorist attacks. More recent incidents involving PTSD include the 2004 Madrid train bombings, the 2004 Indian Ocean earthquake and tsunami, the 2005 London transit bombings, and Hurricane Katrina, which struck the U.S. Gulf Coast in 2005. PTSD can affect people of all ages.

Caregivers of victims of disasters can also be affected by PTSD. A 2007 report at a nursing conference in New Orleans found that nurses and doctors who have been working in that city since Hurricane Katrina struck in 2005 are showing signs of PTSD.

Statistics gathered from past events indicate that the risk of PTSD increases in order of the following factors.

- female gender
- middle-aged (40 to 60 years old)
- little or no experience coping with traumatic events
- ethnic minority
- lower socioeconomic status (SES)
- children in the home
- women with spouses exhibiting PTSD symptoms
- pre-existing psychiatric conditions
- primary exposure to the event including injury, life-threatening situation, and loss
- living in traumatized community

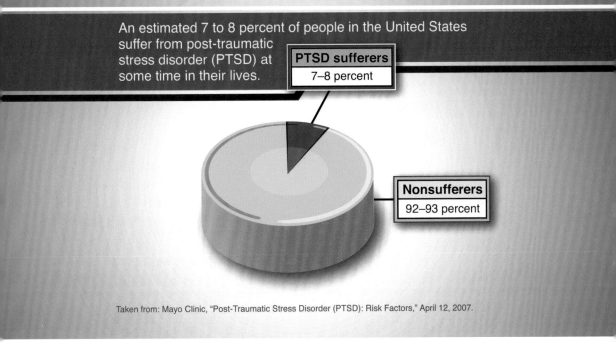

Number of Americans with PTSD

An estimated 7 to 8 percent of people in the United States suffer from post-traumatic stress disorder (PTSD) at some time in their lives.

PTSD sufferers
7–8 percent

Nonsufferers
92–93 percent

Taken from: Mayo Clinic, "Post-Traumatic Stress Disorder (PTSD): Risk Factors," April 12, 2007.

For example, over a third of the Oklahoma City bombing survivors developed PTSD and over half showed signs of anxiety, depression, and alcohol abuse. Over one year later, Oklahomans in general had an increased use of alcohol and tobacco products, as well as PTSD symptoms.

Children are also susceptible to PTSD and their risk is increased exponentially as their exposure to the event increases. Children experiencing abuse, the death of a parent, or those located in a community suffering a traumatic event can develop PTSD. Two years after the Oklahoma City bombing, 16% of children in a 100 mile radius of Oklahoma City with no direct exposure to the bombing had increased symptoms of PTSD. Weak parental response to the event, having a parent suffering from PTSD symptoms, and increased exposure to the event via the media all increase the possibility of the child developing PTSD symptoms.

Causes and Symptoms

Specific causes for the onset of PTSD following a trauma aren't clearly defined, although experts suspect it may be influenced both by the severity of the event, by the person's personality and genetic make-up, and by whether or not the trauma was expected. First response emergency personnel and individuals directly involved in the event or those children and families who have lost loved ones are more likely to experience PTSD. Natural disasters account for about a 5% rate of PTSD, while there is a 50% rate of PTSD among rape and Holocaust survivors.

Media coverage plays a new role in both adult and pediatric onset of PTSD symptoms. The heightened level of news footage of actual traumatic events, such as the Oklahoma City bombing and the terrorist attack on the World Trade Center and the Pentagon, increases the exposure to the violence, injury, and death associated with the event and may reinforce PTSD symptoms in individuals, especially young children who cannot distinguish between the actual event and the repeated viewing of the event in the media.

PTSD symptoms are distinct and prolonged stress reactions that naturally occur during a highly stressful event. Common symptoms are:

- hyperalertness
- fear and anxiety
- nightmares and flashbacks
- sight, sound, and smell recollection
- avoidance of recall situations
- anger and irritability
- guilt
- depression
- increased substance abuse
- negative world view
- decreased sexual activity

Symptoms usually begin within three months of the trauma, although sometimes PTSD doesn't develop until years after the initial trauma occurred. Once the symptoms begin, they may fade away again within six months. Others suffer with the symptoms for far longer and in some cases, the problem may become chronic.

Among the most troubling symptoms of PTSD are flashbacks, which can be triggered by sounds, smells, feelings, or images. During a flashback, the person relives the traumatic event and may completely lose touch with reality, suffering through the trauma for minutes or hours at a time, believing that the traumatizing event is actually happening all over again.

FAST FACT

According to the Mayo Clinic, approximately 5 million Americans suffer from PTSD in any given year.

Necessary Symptoms for Diagnosis

For a diagnosis of PTSD, symptoms must include at least one of the following so-called "intrusive" symptoms:

- flashbacks
- sleep disorders: nightmares or night terrors
- intense distress when exposed to events that are associated with the trauma

In addition, the person must have at least three of the following "avoidance" symptoms that affect interactions with others:

- trying to avoid thinking or feeling about the trauma
- inability to remember the event
- inability to experience emotion, as well as a loss of interest in former pleasures (psychic numbing or blunting)
- a sense of a shortened future

Finally, there must be evidence of increased arousal, including at least two of the following:

- problems falling asleep
- startle reactions: hyperalertness and strong reactions to unexpected noises

- memory problems
- concentration problems
- moodiness
- violence

One of the symptoms helpful in diagnosing PTSD is sleep disorders that include nightmares and night terrors. (© Sebastiano Volponi/ Marka/Alamy)

In addition to the above symptoms, children with PTSD may experience learning disabilities and memory or attention problems. They may become more dependent, anxious, or even self-abusing.

Recovery may be slowed by injuries, damage to property, loss of employment, or other major problems in the community due to disaster.

Not every person who experiences a traumatic event will experience PTSD. A mental health professional will diagnose the condition if the symptoms of stress last for more than a month after a traumatic event. While a formal diagnosis of PTSD is made only in the wake of a severe trauma, it is possible to have a mild PTSD-like reaction following less severe stress.

Treatment and Immediate Care of PTSD

Several factors have shown to be important in the treatment of post-traumatic stress. These include proximity of the treatment to the site of the event, immediate intervention of therapy as soon as possible, and the expectation that the individual will eventually return to more normal functions. The most helpful treatment of prolonged PTSD appears to be a combination of medication along with supportive and cognitive-behavioral therapies.

Immediate intervention is important for individuals directly affected by the traumatic event. Emergency care workers focus on achieving the following during the hours and days following the trauma.

- protect survivors from further danger
- treat immediate injuries
- provide food, shelter, fluids, and clothing
- provide safe zone
- locate separated loved ones
- reconnect loved ones
- provide normal social contact
- help reestablish routines
- help resolve transportation, housing, or other issues caused by disaster
- provide grief counseling, stress reduction, and other consultation to enable survivors and families to return to normal life

As well as providing care to others, emergency personnel often need the same support as the survivors. Operational debriefing is used to organize the emergency response and to disseminate information and sense of purpose to the first responders. Critical Incident Stress Debriefing (CISD) is a formal group invention designed to include various crisis intervention, such as information disbursement, one-on-one counseling, consultation, family crisis intervention, and referrals. CISD is not useful for survivors and is an interim support for first responders until they are able to receive therapy.

Medications and Therapy

Medications used to reduce the symptoms of PTSD include anxiety-reducing medications and antidepressants, especially the selective serotonin reuptake inhibitors (SSRIs) such as fluoxetine (Prozac) and sertraline HCl (Zoloft). In 2001, the U.S. Food and Drug Administration (FDA) approved Zoloft as a long-term treatment for PTSD. In a controlled study, Zoloft was effective in safely improving symptoms of PTSD over a period of 28 weeks and reducing the risk of relapse.

Sleep problems can be lessened with brief treatment with an anti-anxiety drug, such as a benzodiazepine like alprazolam (Xanax), but long-term usage can lead to disturbing side effects, such as increased anger, drug tolerance, dependency, and abuse.

Several types of therapy may be useful and they are often combined in a multi-faceted approach to understand and treat this condition.

- Cognitive-behavioral therapy focuses on changing specific actions and thoughts through repetitive review of traumatic events, identification of negative behaviors and thoughts, and stress management.
- Group therapy has been useful in decreasing psychological distress, depression, and anxiety in some

PTSD sufferers such as sexually abused women and war veterans.

• Psychological debriefing has been widely used to treat victims of natural disasters and other traumatic events such as bombings and workplace shootings, however, recent research shows that psychological debriefing may increase the stress response. Since this type of debriefing focuses on the emotional response of the survivor, it is not recommended for individuals experiencing an extreme level of grief.

Several means of alternative treatment may be helpful in combination with conventional therapy for reduction of the symptoms of post-traumatic stress disorder. These include relaxation training, breathing techniques, spiritual treatment, and drama therapy where the event is re-enacted.

Prognosis and Prevention

The severity of the illness depends in part on whether the trauma was unexpected, the severity of the trauma, how chronic the trauma was (such as for victims of sexual abuse), and the person's readiness to embrace the recovery process. With appropriate medication, emotional support, counseling, and follow-up care, most people show significant improvement. However, prolonged exposure to severe trauma, such as experienced by victims of prolonged physical or sexual abuse and survivors of the Holocaust, may cause permanent psychological scars.

More studies are needed to determine if PTSD can actually be prevented. Some measures that have been explored include controlling exposure to traumatic events through safety and security measures, psychological preparation for individuals who will be exposed to traumatic events (i.e. policemen, paramedics, soldiers), and stress inoculation training (rehearsal of the event with small doses of the stressful situation).

Early History of PTSD in War

Penny Coleman

In the following selection Penny Coleman gives an early history of post-traumatic stress disorder. Covering the Revolutionary War, the Civil War, and World War I, Coleman discusses the terms and conditions given to the precursors of PTSD. Also covered are the prevailing treatments at the time and the attitudes of others toward PTSD sufferers. The beginnings of formal training for psychiatrists in this field are also discussed. Coleman also includes information on the Civil War draft, its inherent unfairness, and the effect it had on soldiers.

Coleman is the widow of a Vietnam veteran and the author of *Flashback: Posttraumatic Stress Disorder, Suicide, and the Lessons of War,* from which this viewpoint is taken.

D uring the American Civil War, it was called "irritable heart" or "nostalgia." In the First World War, it became "shell shock," "hysteria," or "neurasthenia." During World War II and the war in Korea, it was "war neurosis," "battle fatigue," or simply

SOURCE: Penny Coleman, *Flashback: Posttraumatic Stress Disorder, Suicide, and the Lessons of War,* Boston: Beacon Press, 2006.

"exhaustion." When veterans started coming home from Vietnam, it was at first called "Post-Vietnam syndrome." Then, in 1980, with the publication of the third edition of the American Psychiatric Association's *Diagnostic and Statistical Manual of Mental Disorders (DSM-III)*, "post-traumatic stress disorder" (PTSD) entered the official lexicon. The names have changed over time, but the phenomenon they describe has remained distressingly constant: war causes mental illness that is life-altering and, in far too many cases, fatal. . . .

Over time, perhaps the most intractable prejudice has been that those who fall victim to the mental illness caused by war are somehow inherently weak in body or character. That belief has had, and continues to have, many adherents, in spite of evidence that some of the most famous and admired heroes of war, from Ulysses to Audie Murphy, have suffered from symptoms that meet the diagnostic criteria of PTSD. The parallel misconception, that a warrior's success is ensured if his body is strong and his character firm, has likewise plagued and inconvenienced military organizations. If such ideal warriors could be reliably identified, it would certainly make the maintenance of armies more straightforward and the subsequent cost of disability pensions less daunting. Not for lack of trying, no such correlation has been discovered. After 150 years of study, there are still no reliable predictors for who will be affected by their combat experience and under what circumstances. Once affected, there is still no cure. All that is really known is that war is a disease that affects the minds of many who get close to its horrors. The disease can be so painful and debilitating that those afflicted often lose their health, their sanity, their dreams, their families, and often their lives. . . .

The Revolutionary War and PTSD

George Washington's Continental Army, which became the U.S. Army, was plagued with mental health disorders that are recognizably similar to those seen today. Labels of "melancholia" and "insanity" were loosely applied to the most extreme cases, the psychoses, the paralyses, or to those who suffered from invasive flashbacks. "Nostalgia" referred to chronic situational depressions, which were thought to stem primarily from homesickness. "Drunkenness," according to Joseph Lovell (surgeon general, 1817–1828), was responsible for half of the deaths in the U.S. Army during the period of his tenure. Lovell was a temperance advocate who succeeded in abolishing the daily rum ration, which probably makes him a questionable primary source, but it does seem likely that some of the excess consumption, not unlike the self-medication so frequently noted among today's vets, was an attempt to keep demons at bay.

The Civil War and PTSD

The psychic distress of soldiers was a serious but relatively uncomplicated issue for nineteenth-century commanders. During the years of the American Civil War, it was assumed by commanders on both sides that men of strength and character would maintain a "manly" attitude in battle. There was little sympathy in either army for those who did not. Both armies made discharge for psychiatric complaints virtually impossible. If a soldier was beyond masking his traumatic symptoms, he had few options. If he tried to desert and was caught, his comrades would be forced to stand at attention to witness his execution. He would be buried where he fell, and the ground smoothed over his unmarked grave to symbolically erase his existence. He otherwise might apply for a psychiatric discharge and, in some cases, a sympathetic commanding officer would reassign him to light duty. But in applying for relief, he risked calling attention to his distress. If his application was rejected and he could not manage to mask his symptoms, he would be officially labeled a coward or a malingerer. The penalty for cow-

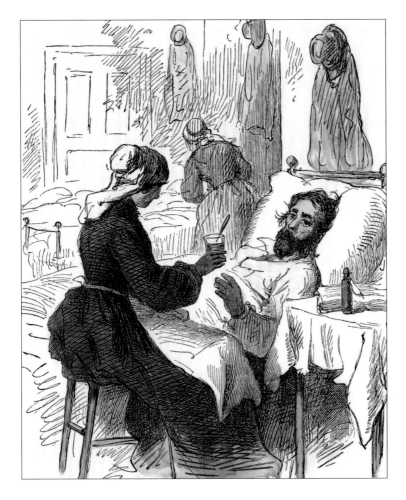

During the American Civil War erroneous diagnoses of PTSD included melancholia, nostalgia, and irritable heart. (© **North Wind Picture Archives/Alamy**)

ardice or malingering was the same as that for desertion. He might just as well have run off in the first place. Executions were intended both to eliminate the contagion of weakness and to terrify the ranks into obedience. Such severe consequences must have discouraged many from seeking help. They certainly encouraged many others to resort to flight.

The Draft Becomes Necessary

At the outset, the social and economic issues over which the war was fought had inspired passion on both sides. Romantic notions of heroism, glory, and honor fed a short-lived frenzy of voluntarism in both the North and the South. By 1862, however, as word of battlefield carnage, rampant disease, and intense hardships became known, the enthusiastic rush to enlist was seriously slowed. The Confederate army was forced to pass a draft law in 1862. The Union followed suit the next year. The laws were unpopular, unwieldy, and patently unfair. They exempted most professionals, and included commutation and substitution clauses, which allowed a draftee to buy his way out of service altogether or pay to send someone else in his place. Pundits North and South began calling it "a rich man's war and a poor man's fight." [Author Jonathan] Shay [who has written two of the most important books about combat-induced trauma] would have called it a betrayal of what's right. The injustice of the draft provoked draft riots in several cities, most notably in New York.

Whether drafted or enlisted, though, the soldiers who fought for the North or for the South were certainly exposed to "events that involved actual or threatened death or serious injury, or a threat to the physical integrity of self or others," and there was adequate cause for a response that "involved intense fear, helplessness, or horror." It is impossible to know how many of the almost 400,000 deserters (about 10 percent of both armies) were running from personal demons, but it was the only recourse, short of execution or suicide, available to those most acutely afflicted.

Studying Combat-Related Stress

Against that background, Dr. Jacob Mendes DaCosta is credited with conducting the first scientific study of combat-related stress. He called the array of symptoms he identified "the irritable heart of a soldier" because so many of his patients complained of shortness of breath, palpitations, anxiety, and chest pain. But generally, soldiers' complaints varied widely, and so did the diagnoses. William Hammond, who was Lincoln's surgeon general, appropriately called the state of nineteenth-century American medicine "the end of the medical Middle Ages." Unlike their European counterparts, who were becoming familiar with the work of [Robert] Koch and [Louis] Pasteur, and who were adopting scientific methodologies to investigate disease, American doctors who served in both armies had virtually no practical training or clinical experience. Their understanding of a soldier's symptoms was therefore based largely on superstition, custom, and a good measure of imagination and the supernatural. What DaCosta diagnosed as irritable heart, another doctor might have called insanity or sunstroke. "Nostalgia," which was a popular diagnostic category at the beginning of the war, implied a weakness of character neither army chose to indulge. After the early years, the diagnosis was firmly discouraged: 5,200 soldiers were hospitalized with "nostalgia" before 1853, but between 1853 and 1865 not a single case was reported. There were, however, 145,000 hospitalizations for constipation, 66,000 for headache, and 58,000 for neuralgia. . . .

Benefits for Disabled Veterans

A tradition of support for disabled veterans dates back to the original colonies. The laws of the Plymouth Colony in 1636 promised soldiers that "if any that shall goe returne maymed [and] hurt he shalbe mayntayned competently by the Colony duringe his life." In 1776, the Continental Congress pensioned veterans who had been disabled in the Revolution. After the Civil War, however, activist veterans organized and lobbied for a pension system that would cover not only those who had been disabled, but all Union Army veterans and their dependents. (Veterans of the Confederate army were not eligible for any federal benefits and had to rely on relatively modest state entitlement programs. By 1891, fully one-third of the federal budget went to military pensions, and eventually, more money was paid out in pensions than the $8 billion spent on prosecuting the war itself.

In the midst of all that generosity, those who suffered from "irritable heart" or "nostalgia" found it virtually impossible to qualify for support of any kind. The Pension Bureau required proof that symptoms had originated in service, especially if, as was often the case, the onset of symptoms was delayed. Proof was hard to come by. If, after years of intolerable battlefield nightmares, a disturbed veteran turned to drink, he was held responsible for his "vicious habits" and rejected. If he used drugs to quell his violent outbursts, he would likewise be rejected. Vicious habits, to the Victorian mind, were an indication of moral laxity. They were considered indicators of intemperance, and intemperance was believed to upset the delicate systemic balance on which sanity rests. Acknowledgment of any form of "self-pollution" rendered the claimant morally unworthy of official support. As in the aftermath of future wars, those who had been psychically damaged, those whose wounds did not show, those who were least able to advocate for themselves, were afforded the least support and compassion. . . .

Shell Shock and World War I

At the outbreak of the First World War, the horrors of trench warfare produced psychiatric casualties in shocking numbers. Men in the trenches were trapped below ground level, often for weeks at a time, in a world bounded by cold, mud, rats, lice, dysentery, and the shrieks of both deadly incoming artillery and dying comrades. They were immobile, helpless, and passive witnesses to what those arbitrary shells did to the men around them, imagining what the next might do to them. The 1,906 British cases of "behavior disorder without physical cause" admitted to hospitals in 1914 grew to 20,327 in 1915, or 9 percent of battle casualties. Then on July 1, 1916, the very first day of the horrific battle fought in the Somme Valley, 60,000 of the 110,000 British troops who attacked a mere six German divisions were either killed or wounded. Historian Paul Fussell gives full credit for the slaughter that became known among the troops as the "Great F--- Up" to Sir Douglas Haig, commander of the British forces. According to Fussell, Haig believed that his working-class army was "too simple and too animal to cross the space between the opposing trenches in any way except in full daylight and aligned in rows or 'waves.'" For the next four months, Haig held to his plan until freezing mud put an end to the massacre. By that time, the Somme had claimed another half-million British casualties.

A Toll on the Mind

It is hardly surprising that such madness would take a toll not just of bodies, but of minds. At times, more than 50 percent of the evacuated casualties were psychiatric. The response of the director-general of medical services was that "wastage" was simply not to be evacuated "unless there are definite lesions and symptoms which require prolonged hospital treatment." Initially, the British psychiatrists who saw some of those first psychiatric casualties, specifically Dr. Charles Myers, looked for a physical

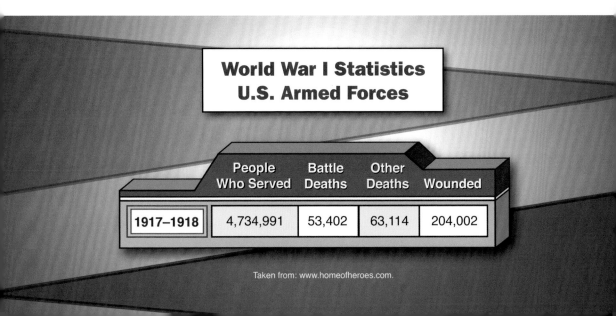

**World War I Statistics
U.S. Armed Forces**

	People Who Served	Battle Deaths	Other Deaths	Wounded
1917–1918	4,734,991	53,402	63,114	204,002

Taken from: www.homeofheroes.com.

explanation, hypothesizing that the constant and random concussion of bursting shells caused actual lesions in the brain. Myers called it "shell shock." The name stuck, in spite of the fact that subsequent autopsy results failed to bear out his theory.

Military Discipline of Field Soldiers

With the idea of brain lesions discredited, doctors once again sought explanations for traumatic symptoms in the moral character of the individual. . . . The authorities dusted off the terms "malingerer" and "coward" and used them to justify court-martial or dishonorable discharge. As during the American Civil War, many who broke down were summarily shot. Denis Winter, in *Death's Men*, quotes one hard-boiled division commander who insisted that there was no fear in his division because, at the first symptoms, he tied the coward to the front-line barbed wire for thirty seconds "with most effective results." Thirty seconds was generally adequate time for a sniper from the other side to shift what might have been a psychiatric casualty statistic into the medical, if not the mortality, column—killing, as it were, two birds with one stone. It was finally, just "a matter of luck," as one military psychiatrist put it, whether a distressed soldier was hospitalized for shell shock or shot for cowardice.

The callous attitudes that shaped extreme military discipline in the field were mirrored behind the lines in the treatment centers of "traditionalist" military psychiatrists. Clovis Vincent in France and Lewis Yealland in England were particularly infamous. Both practiced a form of faradic stimulation, or electric shock, applied to whichever part of the body was refusing to cooperate. Used in combination with threats and humiliation, the treatment was patently cruel, exquisitely painful, and finally unreliable. It was also rarely practiced on officers. "Torpillage" (literally "torpedoing"), as it was known in France, was discredited after a patient, fearing he was about to be electrocuted, struck Vincent in the face. The patient was convicted of assault by a military tribunal, but the conviction was reported in the popular press. Public revulsion resulted in the sentence being overturned, and the barbarous practice fell out of favor.

Simplified Treatment Becomes More Widespread

Between the ultimate discipline of the military hard-liners, the punitive practices of the psychiatric traditionalists, and the narrow Freudian construction, there gradually emerged a more moderate group of "shell shock" doctors looking to develop a theory of practice that acknowledged compassion and reason, but within the bounds of efficacy demanded by the military. Myers, no longer believing in a physical explanation, and by then consulting psychiatrist to the British Army, instituted a new policy to deal with combat-related stress: prompt, forward, and simplified treatment.

If men were not to be evacuated, they would have to be treated close to the front. That necessity fortuitously conflated with Myers's conviction that time and distance tend to dim a soldier's group loyalty and identification. If, as Myers believed, loyalty to one's comrades was central to a soldier's capacity to withstand horror, terror, and death, then separation from those comrades, be it in distance or time, would lessen those bonds. Evacuation to a safe and comfortable rear hospital, he reasoned, would allow individuality to reassert itself. Self-preservation would drown out loyalty.

Myers's insistence on a "simplified" or short-term treatment was only partly dictated by logistics. He had also observed the tendency of soldiers to use lengthy analytical exploration to convince themselves that they had good reason for having reached the limits of their endurance. Under Myers's tenure, doctors were taught never to use the words "shell shock" when speaking with their patients. The validation implicit in a clinical-sounding diagnosis seemed to encourage, rather than ease, their symptoms. Prompt, forward, simplified treatment amounted to a good night's rest, a hot meal, and some positive morale boosting, all with the emphatically expressed assumption that the soldier would soon return to the lines. The goal of treatment was therefore the restoration of psychic defenses for the purpose of return to combat duty. Whether or not such repressive or suppressive therapy was in the interest of the soldier, it was certainly successful by military standards—in the short term. Sigmund Freud is said to have likened the role of the military psychiatrist to that "of a machine gun behind the front line, that of driving back those who fled.

> **FAST FACT**
>
> A 2005 study of Korean War veterans in Australia showed that nearly 33 percent experienced symptoms that matched the criteria for PTSD.

Training for Psychiatrists

The possibility that Americans might find themselves involved in this war prompted the first formal training in psychiatry for regular army medical officers. By 1915, that training consisted of four clinical sessions at the Government Hospital and lectures in military law and malingering, demanding a total investment of twenty-four hours of an officer's time. further measure of the respect accorded psychiatry in the U.S. Army when the Americans joined the war in 1917 is that the man who was put in charge of the soldiers' mental health, Thomas Salmon, was a bacteriologist by training who had acquired what he knew about psychiatry screening immigrants arriving at Ellis Island. By the time the Americans joined the war in 1917, the British and French experience with the efficacy of brief forward treatment had been demonstrated, and it was instituted in the American army with gratifying success. There were echelons of treatment centers, providing progressively longer and more intensive care at increasing distance from the front. Rest, warmth, food, and encouragement were the curatives of choice. Staff were ordered to use the British label "N.Y.D.N."—not yet diagnosed (nervous)—instead of dramatic labels like "shell shock," to avoid the frightening suggestion of a brain injury. They were, furthermore, instructed to emphasize the glorious traditions of the military, the opportunity to claim the honors and rewards of victory, and a place in the "family" unit. Evacuation meant separation from the paternal officer and brother soldier, and finally becoming that most unhappy of mortals, the lone casualty. It was in a sense a desertion, since it left comrades to carry on alone. Regardless of whether we consider that script emotional blackmail, it was certainly effective. Seventy percent returned to their units in less than five days, and over half of the remaining 30 percent, within two weeks.

PTSD Treatment in Children

Mark Goulston

PTSD treatment in children is a field of study that has been largely ignored. In the following selection Mark Goulston gives information on several of the most effective therapies available for children, including cognitive behavior therapy (CBT), eye movement desensitization and reprocessing therapy (EMDR), and play therapy. Goulson discusses the benefits of each therapy, along with specifics on how each therapy works. Also covered are the advantages and disadvantages of PTSD medications used in children.

Goulston is a clinical psychiatrist and a fellow of the American Psychiatric Association.

S ome aspects of medicine are so well studied that it's almost silly. (Do we *really* need another study saying that french fries are bad for you?) Other areas, however, are largely unexplored territory. Unfortunately, childhood PTSD falls into that category.

SOURCE: Mark Goulston, *Post-Traumatic Stress Disorder for Dummies*, Indianapolis: Wiley Publishing, Inc., 2008. Copyright © 2008 by Wiley Publishing, Inc. Reproduced with permission of John Wiley & Sons, Inc.

The research on what works and what doesn't for treating PTSD in kids is skimpier than it should be, but doctors and therapists can draw some good conclusions about the most common approaches. In the following sections, I discuss these approaches and explain what professionals know and don't know about their effectiveness. . . .

Cognitive Behavioral Therapy

Cognitive Behavioral Therapy (CBT) is the most popular and well-validated approach for treating PTSD in adults. (This form of treatment is also referred to as *trauma-based CBT* because it asks patients to re-experience their trauma to overcome it.) Studies strongly indicate that CBT is also an excellent therapy for children. . . .

Just like adult therapy, CBT for children starts by teaching children techniques for relaxation and stress management; then it helps them confront their trauma and make sense of what happened to them. CBT therapists who work with children, however, modify their techniques to take the following factors into account:

- Age and developmental level: CBT can work for children as young as 3 years old, but therapists often use techniques for children that differ from the ones they use for adults. A CBT therapist may ask a 6-year-old to act out the trauma with dolls or to draw pictures of his trauma, as well as describe the scene verbally. The therapist may also use role-playing to allow the child to understand the trauma from different people's points of view.
- The role of parents: Therapists who work with kids realize that parents are the most important people in a child's life and that they're crucial to the child's success in healing from PTSD. Thus, therapists include Mom, Dad, or both in many sessions. . . .

PTSD and Children

Incidence of PTSD among children who have experienced a traumatic event.

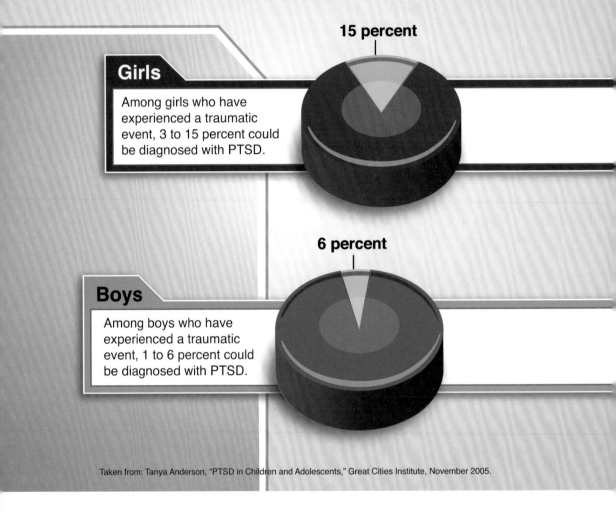

15 percent

Girls

Among girls who have experienced a traumatic event, 3 to 15 percent could be diagnosed with PTSD.

6 percent

Boys

Among boys who have experienced a traumatic event, 1 to 6 percent could be diagnosed with PTSD.

Taken from: Tanya Anderson, "PTSD in Children and Adolescents," Great Cities Institute, November 2005.

How CBT Benefits Kids and Teens

As your child works through her trauma and figures out how to see it through new eyes, her initial fear and distress will fade, and she'll become more confident, happy, and ready to face the future. Her therapist can help her do this by zeroing in on these goals in particular:

- Helping her learn not to catastrophize events in [her] life so she won't be scared all the time; for instance, a therapist can help your child realize that
- If Daddy's feeling a little under the weather, it doesn't mean that he's having another heart attack.
- Cloudy skies usually don't mean that another tornado is on the way.
- Eliminating any misplaced guilt she feels as a result of the trauma
- Empowering her to feel strong and capable so that she's less fearful of potential future crises

Scientific Support for CBT

Most research on the effects of CBT involves adults instead of children, but the number of pediatric studies is growing, and the results strongly support the effectiveness of this approach. Following are samples of recent findings:

- A 2006 study published by Ioanna Giannopoulou and colleagues in *Clinical Child Psychology and Psychiatry* followed 20 children who developed PTSD after a large earthquake in Athens, Greece. The researchers found that CBT resulted in a significant reduction in overall PTSD symptoms as well as symptoms of depression. Effects were long-lasting, with the children continuing to show positive effects four years after therapy.
- A 2006 study by Esther Deblinger and colleagues, published in the *Journal of the American Academy of Child and Adolescent Psychiatry,* involved 183 children who developed symptoms of PTSD after being sexually abused. The researchers compared CBT with a treatment called child-centered therapy (CCT), which doesn't specifically address the child's trauma. Their findings: Children treated with CBT had significantly fewer symptoms of PTSD and experienced less shame as a result of their trauma than the children who participated in CCT.

• A 2005 review in the journal *Depression and Anxiety* by Gili Adler-Nevo and Katharina Manassis compared three treatments for children with PTSD resulting from a single trauma; the report concluded that although all three therapies are effective, CBT has the best scientific support. (For info on the other two therapies, EMDR and play therapy, see the following sections.)

The National Center for Posttraumatic Stress Disorder recommends CBT for traumatized kids and teens, concluding that "this is the most effective approach for treating children." The Chadwick Center for Children and Families also highly recommended CBT in a comprehensive 2004 report on the best practices in the treatment of children traumatized by abuse. . . .

Eye Movement Desensitization and Reprocessing (EMDR) Therapy

EMDR is very similar to CBT because it asks a participant to re-experience her trauma in the safety of a therapy setting. A patient participating in EMDR, however, recalls the trauma silently in short segments. At the same time, she uses her eyes to follow the therapist's finger as he moves it slowly and steadily from side to side.

Therapists use the same approach for children and adults when offering EMDR treatment, but they sometimes modify sessions in these ways:

• To hold a younger child's visual attention, the therapist may move an eye-catching finger puppet from side to side instead of moving a finger alone.
• Sessions tend to be shorter than those for adults. Sessions for children usually last about 45 minutes at most.
• Therapy for children often involves fewer sessions because children appear to react to the therapy more quickly than adults do.

The Inside Story on EMDR's Effectiveness for Kids

The scientific literature on EMDR for children is small but growing, and early results suggest that it's just as effective as CBT (which isn't surprising, because the two approaches are very similar). Here are some findings:

- In a 2002 study reported by Claude Chemtob and colleagues in the *Journal of Clinical Psychology*, researchers used EMDR to treat 32 children who still exhibited PTSD one year after a disaster. After treatment, the children showed significant improvements in PTSD symptoms, anxiety, and depression, and they continued to experience these positive changes at a six-month follow-up.
- A study by Guinevere Tufnell, published in *Clinical Child Psychology and Psychiatry* in 2005, followed four preteens treated with EMDR for PTSD symptoms. In all four cases, the children's symptoms were well-controlled within two to four sessions. A follow-up six months later showed that the children continued to do well.

EMDR has other advantages: It often works quickly, which can translate into faster healing as well as less expense for parents; and it's a good approach for very shy children or those with limited verbal skills because it asks children to recall their trauma silently rather than out loud.

Play Therapy

Adults think of play as fun, but for kids, it's also a powerful tool for expressing love, rage, fear, and other very big emotions. For this reason, therapists often use play to explore what's going on in the mind of a child who's too young to describe his inner feelings in words. . . .

An adult knows about 50,000 words, but a child of 5 or 6 knows only about 5,000. What's more, an adult's vocabulary includes lots of expressions to describe emotions (such as "I was flabbergasted!" or "I was tense and on edge, like I was overcaffeinated"), whereas a young child's toolbox of words to describe his feelings is pretty limited. Because he has a small set of words to describe a big event, a young child can't always tell a parent or a therapist how he feels after a trauma changes his life.

Play therapy gets around the language problem by giving a child other outlets for expressing himself, including dolls, puppets, stuffed animals, toy houses and cars, sand, water, paint, clay, and crayons. Watching a child's play, a therapist can gently guide him to air his feelings. Here's an example of how this approach works:

Through play therapy a therapist can often encourage children to talk about their traumatic experiences. (John Cole/Photo Researchers, Inc.)

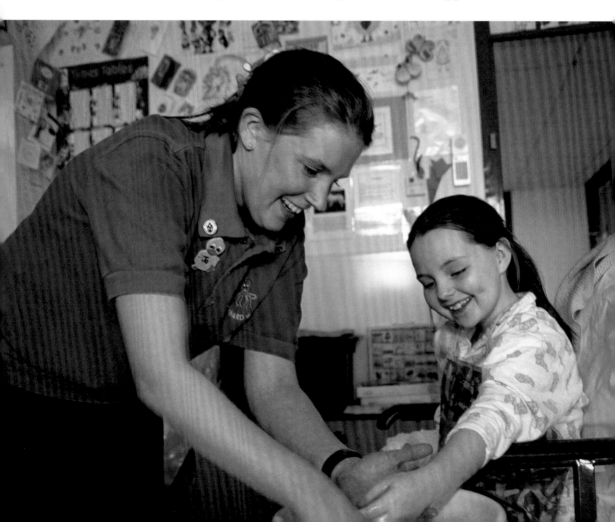

- If the child repeatedly crashes two toy cars together, a therapist may ask, "How do the people in those cars feel when they crash together?"
- If the child draws a picture of a person screaming, the therapist may ask, "What is happening that's scaring that person?"

Gradually, a therapist can get a child to open up more and more about the trauma he experienced. The therapist has two goals in this process: to understand the child's thoughts and feelings and to use play to guide him to explore new ways of thinking and feeling.

A child traumatized by a dog attack, for example, may spontaneously reenact the trauma by using a toy dog to attack a doll named Charlie over and over. The therapist may respond in these ways:

- First, she may ask how the doll feels when the attack occurs. ("Is Charlie scared when the dog bites him on the foot?")
- Next, she may ask how the doll feels after the trauma occurs. ("What happens later, when a dog comes up to Charlie in the park?")
- Eventually, she may have the child experiment with different ways the doll could feel and act now. ("Here's a little friendly dog that's very different from that big mean one. This dog is very kind and gentle, and he's on a leash, so he can't run up and jump on Charlie. This dog really likes Charlie and wants to be his friend. Do you think that Charlie will be able to pet him?")

Play therapy can also be effective for older children who have trouble opening up verbally about their trauma. Doctors sometimes recommend this approach for children as old as 12.

The Bottom Line on Play Therapy

Play therapy is one of the oldest treatments for traumatized children, but judging its overall effectiveness is hard because most studies of this approach involve only one or two children. These small case studies don't offer much insight into how useful this approach is for kids in general.

In general play therapy appears to be less effective than trauma-based CBT or EMDR. . . . It's an excellent choice, however, for children who are too young or frightened to benefit from CBT or EMDR and for kids with very limited verbal skills. It's also a gentle and nonthreatening approach for many children with developmental disabilities. . . .

FAST FACT

EMDR is gaining popularity as a children's PTSD therapy because it can be used when individuals have limited verbal skills.

Medications

Just like adults, children with PTSD sometimes benefit greatly from medications. For a child who's out of control, the right medication sometimes puts on the brakes long enough for psychological therapies to take hold. . . .

Doctors prescribe many of the same medications for children and teens, but these drugs can be far riskier for the younger set than for adults. Here's why:

- Researchers tend to study the effects of psychiatric drugs on adults more thoroughly than they study these drugs' effects on children. As a result, proof that a drug is relatively safe for an adult doesn't necessarily translate into proof that it's safe for a kid.
- Kids aren't just little grownups when it comes to medications. Because children are growing and changing, their metabolism and brain function can be very different—which means that drugs can affect them differently than they affect adults.

As a result, psychiatric drugs can have serious and sometimes surprising effects in kids, especially when a doctor combines two or more of these medications. . . .

In particular, be extremely cautious if your child's doctor recommends antidepressants. Some of these drugs now carry "black box" warnings—the strongest warnings that the U.S. Food and Drug Administration can require—cautioning that the drugs may cause suicidal thoughts or behavior in children. Doctors are still debating whether antidepressants actually increase or decrease the overall risk of suicide in young people, but be aware that this is a potential concern. . . .

If you decide that medication is a good option, be sure that your child receives regular medical monitoring. Frequent tests can help prevent side effects or catch them at an early stage.

Also, realize that medications—even when they work wonders—should supplement psychological interventions instead of being a primary or sole treatment.

PTSD Treatment in Adults

National Center for Posttraumatic Stress Disorder

In the following article the National Center for Posttraumatic Stress Disorder discusses the available treatment for adult PTSD. One of the most effective types of counseling is cognitive behavioral therapy, or CBT. Within this category are several different types of therapies, including exposure therapy and eye movement desensitization and reprocessing therapy. Also discussed are several kinds of alternative counseling, including group therapy, family therapy, and brief psychodynamic psychotherapy. Other aspects of adult treatment are also covered.

The National Center for Posttraumatic Stress Disorder is an office in the U.S. Department of Veterans Affairs, a federal agency that provides benefits and medical care to American veterans.

Today, there are good treatments available for PTSD. When you have PTSD dealing with the past can be hard. Instead of telling others how you feel, you may keep your feelings bottled up. But talking with a therapist can help you get better.

SOURCE: "Treatment of PTSD," National Center for Posttraumatic Stress Disorder, May 31, 2007. Reproduced by permission.

Cognitive-behavioral therapy (CBT) is one type of counseling. It appears to be the most effective type of counseling for PTSD. There are different types of cognitive behavioral therapies such as cognitive therapy and exposure therapy. There is also a similar kind of therapy called eye movement desensitization and reprocessing (EMDR) that is used for PTSD. Medications have also been shown to be effective. A type of drug known as a selective serotonin reuptake inhibitor (SSRI), which is also used for depression, is effective for PTSD.

Cognitive Behavioral Therapy

In cognitive therapy, your therapist helps you understand and change how you think about your trauma and its aftermath. Your goal is to understand how certain thoughts about your trauma cause you stress and make your symptoms worse.

You will learn to identify thoughts about the world and yourself that are making you feel afraid or upset. With the help of your therapist, you will learn to replace these thoughts with more accurate and less distressing thoughts. You also learn ways to cope with feelings such as anger, guilt, and fear.

After a traumatic event, you might blame yourself for things you couldn't have changed. For example, a soldier may feel guilty about decisions he or she had to make during war. Cognitive therapy, a type of CBT, helps you understand that the traumatic event you lived through was not your fault.

Exposure Therapy

In exposure therapy your goal is to have less fear about your memories. It is based on the idea that people learn to fear thoughts, feelings, and situations that remind them of a past traumatic event.

By talking about your trauma repeatedly with a therapist, you'll learn to get control of your thoughts

Common Causes of PTSD

Risk of developing PTSD following various types of trauma:

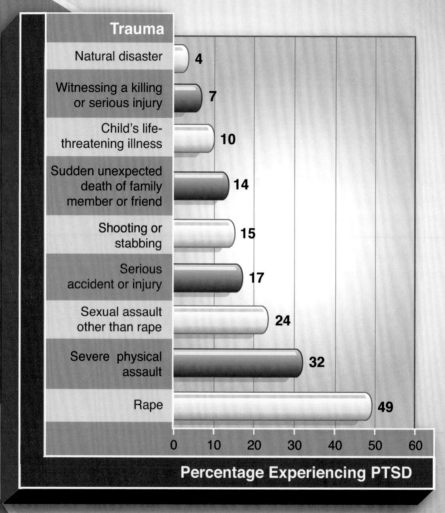

Trauma	Percentage Experiencing PTSD
Natural disaster	4
Witnessing a killing or serious injury	7
Child's life-threatening illness	10
Sudden unexpected death of family member or friend	14
Shooting or stabbing	15
Serious accident or injury	17
Sexual assault other than rape	24
Severe physical assault	32
Rape	49

Taken from: Mark Goulston, *Post-Traumatic Stress Disorder for Dummies.* Hoboken, NJ: John Wiley & Sons, Inc., 2008.

and feelings about the trauma. You'll learn that you do not have to be afraid of your memories. This may be hard at first. It might seem strange to think about stressful things on purpose. But you'll feel less overwhelmed over time.

With the help of your therapist, you can change how you react to the stressful memories. Talking in a place where you feel secure makes this easier.

You may focus on memories that are less upsetting before talking about worse ones. This is called "desensitization," and it allows you to deal with bad memories a little bit at a time. Your therapist also may ask you to remember a lot of bad memories at once. This is called "flooding," and it helps you learn not to feel overwhelmed.

You also may practice different ways to relax when you're having a stressful memory. Breathing exercises are sometimes used for this.

Eye Movement Desensitization and Reprocessing

Eye movement desensitization and reprocessing (EMDR) is a fairly new therapy for PTSD. Like other kinds of counseling, it can help change how you react to memories of your trauma.

While talking about your memories, you'll focus on distractions like eye movements, hand taps, and sounds. For example, your therapist will move his or her hand near your face, and you'll follow this movement with your eyes.

Experts are still learning how EMDR works. Studies have shown that it may help you have fewer PTSD symptoms. But research also suggests that the eye movements are not a necessary part of the treatment.

Medication Used in Treatment

Selective serotonin reuptake inhibitors (SSRIs) are a type of antidepressant medicine. These can help you feel less sad and worried. They appear to be helpful, and for some people they are very effective. SSRIs include citalopram (Celexa), fluoxetine (such as Prozac), paroxetine (Paxil), and sertraline (Zoloft).

Chemicals in your brain affect the way you feel. When you have depression you may not have enough of a chemical called serotonin. SSRIs raise the level of serotonin in your brain.

There are other medications that have been used with some success. Talk to your doctor about which medications are right for you.

In addition to CBT and SSRIs, some other kinds of counseling may be helpful in your recovery from PTSD.

Group Therapy

In group therapy PTSD sufferers can talk about their trauma with others who share similar experiences.
(© Bill Bachmann/Alamy)

Many people want to talk about their trauma with others who have had similar experiences. In group therapy, you talk with a group of people who also have been through a trauma and who have PTSD. Sharing your story with others may help you feel more comfortable talking about your trauma. This can help you cope with your symptoms, memories, and other parts of your life.

Group therapy helps you build relationships with others who understand what you've been through. You learn to deal with emotions such as shame, guilt, anger, rage, and fear. Sharing with the group also can help you build self-confidence and trust. You'll learn to focus on your present life, rather than feeling overwhelmed by the past.

Brief Psychodynamic Psychotherapy

In this type of therapy, you learn ways of dealing with emotional conflicts caused by your trauma. This therapy helps you understand how your past affects the way you feel now.

Your therapist can help you:
- Identify what triggers your stressful memories and other symptoms.
- Find ways to cope with intense feelings about the past.
- Become more aware of your thoughts and feelings, so you can change your reactions to them.
- Raise your self-esteem.

Family Therapy

PTSD can impact your whole family. Your kids or your partner may not understand why you get angry sometimes, or why you're under so much stress. They may feel scared, guilty, or even angry about your condition.

Family therapy is a type of counseling that involves your whole family. A therapist helps you and your family communicate, maintain good relationships, and cope with tough emotions. Your family can learn more about PTSD and how it is treated.

In family therapy, each person can express his or her fears and concerns. It's important to be honest about your feelings and to listen to others. You can talk about your PTSD symptoms and what triggers them. You also can discuss the important parts of your treatment and recovery. By doing this, your family will be better prepared to help you.

You may consider having individual therapy for your PTSD symptoms and family therapy to help you with your relationships.

Other Treatment Aspects

For some people, treatment for PTSD can last 3 to 6 months. If you have other mental health problems as well as PTSD, treatment for PTSD may last for 1 to 2 years or longer.

It is very common to have PTSD at the same time as another mental health problem. Depression, alcohol or substance abuse problems, panic disorder, and other anxiety disorders often occur along with PTSD. In many cases, the PTSD treatments described above will also help with the other disorders. The best treatment results occur when both PTSD and the other problems are treated together rather than one after the other.

FAST FACT

More than 70 percent of Americans will suffer a traumatic event at some point in their lives.

The Therapy Process

When you begin therapy, you and your therapist should decide together what goals you hope to reach in therapy. Not every person with PTSD will have the same treatment goals. For instance, not all people with PTSD are focused on reducing their symptoms.

Some people want to learn the best way to live with their symptoms and how to cope with other problems associated with PTSD. Perhaps you want to feel less guilt and sadness? Perhaps you would like to work on improving your relationships at work, or communication issues with your friends and family.

Your therapist should help you decide which of these goals seems most important to you, and he or she should discuss with you which goals might take a long time to achieve.

What to Expect from the Therapist

Your therapist should give you a good explanation for the therapy. You should understand why your therapist is choosing a specific treatment for you, how long they expect the therapy to last, and how they see if it is working.

The two of you should agree at the beginning that this plan makes sense for you and what you will do if it does not seem to be working. If you have any questions about the treatment your therapist should be able to answer them.

You should feel comfortable with your therapist and feel you are working as a team to tackle your problems. It can be difficult to talk about painful situations in your life, or about traumatic experiences that you have had. Feelings that emerge during therapy can be scary and challenging. Talking with your therapist about the process of therapy, and about your hopes and fears in regards to therapy, will help make therapy successful.

If you do not like your therapist or feel that the therapist is not helping you, it might be helpful to talk with another professional. In most cases, you should tell your therapist that you are seeking a second opinion.

Healing Combat Trauma

Aphrodite Matsakis

In the following article author Aphrodite Matsakis discusses the views of psychiatrist Judith Herman on dealing with and healing from a traumatic event. Herman advocates a three-stage recovery process: creating safety, uncovering and recalling the trauma, and reconnecting with others. According to Matsakis, creating safety involves bringing about internal and external safety, and reconnecting involves making new connections with oneself and with others. Also covered is the time involved in healing from this type of trauma.

Matsakis is a counseling psychologist and author of books and articles on various psychological topics.

In her landmark book, *Trauma and Recovery*, Dr. Judith Herman describes healing from trauma as a three-stage process involving the following:

SOURCE: Aphrodite Matsakis, *Back from the Front: Combat Trauma, Love, and the Family*, Baltimore: Sidran Institute Press, 2007. Copyright © 2007 by Sidran Institute Press. All rights reserved. Reproduced by permission.

1. Creating safety (making one's world as safe as possible);
2. Uncovering the trauma and feeling the feelings; and
3. Reconnecting (with one's self and others).

Stage 1: Creating Safety

External safety. One aspect of safety is external: A vet [military veteran] cannot begin to heal from his psychic or spiritual wounds if he is still being wounded. If he is in an abusive or exploitative living or work situation or is otherwise living in danger, he will need to take steps to create a safe living environment. The same holds true for you, his partner. For example, if you are expressing your frustrations by driving an unsafe car or by engaging in other risky behaviors, then you need to take corrective action.

Internal safety. Another aspect of safety is internal. A vet needs to feel safe with his thoughts, feelings, and behaviors before he can contemplate his war experiences. When the symptoms of PTSD, depression, or some other traumatic reactions make a veteran feel out of control, those symptoms need to be his primary area of concentration. In stage 2, the focus of the therapy is helping the veteran feel safe within himself by getting control over nightmares, intrusive thoughts, flashbacks, insomnia, depression, or any addiction, such as alcohol or drug abuse, gambling, or an eating disorder. It is not wise to begin the unsettling process of reexamining war experiences and the other stages of the healing process unless the vet feels he can exert at least some control over the symptoms that are creating the most havoc in his life. . . .

Under professional supervision—in addition to "talk therapy" with a competent therapist—medication, an alternative treatment, or learning and mastering some of the available coping techniques are often helpful. However, coping techniques, such as muscle relaxation or visualization, must be practiced and mastered.

Stage 2: Uncovering the Trauma and Feeling the Feelings

Only when a vet has established a certain degree of internal and external safety can he then safely proceed to the second stage of healing, which involves remembering the trauma and feeling the feelings associated with the trauma. The major feelings that need to be dealt with are anger, guilt, and grief.

For some vets, war experiences are quite vivid; for others, only partially remembered; for still others, almost

Psychologist Abraham Maslow's Hierarchy of Human Needs

Self Actual- ization

Esteem Needs
Self-esteem
Recognition
Status

Social Needs
Sense of belonging
Love

Safety Needs
Security
Protection

Physiological Needs
Hunger
Thirst

Taken from: www.ptsdforum.org.

totally repressed. The veteran's traumatic memories are not repressed because he is, or was, neurotic, but because by definition a trauma is an event that so overwhelms an individual that he cannot accept it as happening to him. Even if he remembers many of his experiences, it is the specific events that were especially traumatic or life changing which need to be brought into conscious awareness, then shared in group or individual therapy. The veteran does not need to remember all of his traumas. However, he needs to remember enough of his war experiences so that he can make sense of his symptoms and understand his emotional and other reactions to current reminders of the war and other aspects of his life today.

> **FAST FACT**
>
> The Department of Veterans Affairs reports that mental health cases among war veterans grew 58 percent between June 2006 and June 2007.

Recalling Trauma

It can be extremely therapeutic for some vets to recall previously forgotten or dimly remembered traumatic experiences and share them with others. However, it is also necessary for a vet to rethink or re-evaluate his combat experiences and to understand the meaning of these events in his life. He especially needs to re-evaluate incidents about which he feels guilt or shame regarding a particular feeling, thought, action or inaction, or error in judgment. In many cases, the veteran fails to acknowledge how the complex and ambiguous nature of combat may have contributed to his behavior. A therapist or members of a veterans group can help the vet evaluate these and other critical incidents more objectively.

As a result, a vet may come to realize that perhaps he was not such a coward after all or perhaps his friends would have been killed anyway. If indeed his cowardice or viciousness resulted in an irreversible tragedy, the vet must feel the pain of his guilt directly rather than run from it. With the help and support of a therapist or a veterans group, he can try to learn to forgive himself. "The message is . . ." [according to Herman] that many veterans ". . . did the best job in the situation that could have been done considering the circumstances and the resources available in the situation."

In addition to reformulating his war experiences mentally, the veteran needs to take steps toward feeling the feelings associated with these experiences, feelings that were not felt at the time these particular events occurred. Repressed grief and repressed anger are usually the two major emotions that emerge. As these and other emotions rise to the surface, a vet can be helped in learning how to direct the powerful energy contained in some of his emotions into constructive, rather than destructive, channels. Often at this point, the veteran may begin to make associations between past and present and see how his war experiences and his reactions to them have impacted his life, positively as well as negatively.

Stage 3: Reconnecting with Self and Others

The third stage in healing involves re-establishing human ties. When a vet's life was dominated by combat memories or by an addiction or lifestyle that helped numb him to the effects of combat, most likely he did not have much time or energy to devote to relationships. Yet problems with his family, friendships, or love life may have caused him to withdraw or contributed to his turning to alcohol, drugs, food, gambling, or sex as a substitute for meaningful human contact. Once he has some understanding of his trauma and some control over his symptoms, including any addiction he may have had, he may be ready to begin to reestablish some old relationships and even consider building new ones.

The third stage also involves reconnecting with some of his former goals and values and having increased energy for present-day life and future plans. For some vets, healing involves a spiritual or moral dimension, as well as

an emotional one. For these veterans, stage 3 may involve an attempt to re-evaluate or perhaps even reconnect with their former faith or with their spirituality. Spiritually, some vets seek absolution for their actions. For some vets, group therapy is the route to self-forgiveness. For others, the assistance of a rabbi, priest, minister, or other clergyperson or spiritual leader is needed. The need for absolution may also result in the veteran becoming involved in various "survivor missions" (such as helping other veterans or war refugees) or in other charitable works.

The third stage of PTSD treatment involves reconnecting with family, friends, and oneself. (**AP Images**)

PTSD Research

Associated Press

In the following article the author discusses new research that shows genetics may play a role in post-traumatic stress disorder. According to researchers, a stress-related gene variation has been found that may help explain why a similar traumatic event will lead to post-traumatic stress disorder in one individual and not in another. In cases of prolonged abuse—that is, child abuse—individuals with this certain gene variation are much more likely to suffer PTSD. Research is also showing that critical periods in childhood help shape the body's stress response system.

The Associated Press is one of the largest news organizations providing print, photos, graphics, audio, and video.

Groundbreaking research suggests genes help explain why some people can recover from a traumatic event while others suffer post-traumatic stress disorder.

SOURCE: "Genes Help Explain Post-Traumatic Puzzle," msnbc.com, March 18, 2008. Copyright © 2008 The Associated Press. Republished with permission.

Though preliminary, the study provides insight into a condition expected to strike increasing numbers of military veterans returning from combat in Iraq and Afghanistan, one health expert said.

Stress-Related Gene Variations

Researchers found that specific variations in a stress-related gene appeared to be influenced by trauma at a young age—in this case child abuse. That interaction strongly increased the chances for adult survivors of abuse to develop signs of PTSD.

Among adult survivors of severe child abuse, those with the specific gene variations scored more than twice as high on a scale of post-traumatic stress, compared with those without the variations. The worse the abuse, the stronger the risk in people with those gene variations.

The study of 900 adults is among the first to show that genes can be influenced by outside, nongenetic factors to trigger signs of PTSD. It is the largest of just two reports to show molecular evidence of a genetic influence on PTSD.

"We have known for over a decade, from twin studies, that genetic factors play a role in vulnerability to developing PTSD, but have had little success in identifying specific genetic variants that increase risk of the disorder," said Karestan Koenen, a Harvard psychologist doing similar research. She was not involved in the new study.

The results suggest that there are critical periods in childhood when the brain is vulnerable "to outside influences that can shape the developing stress-response system," said Emory University researcher and study co-author Dr. Kerry Ressler.

The study appears in [the March 19, 2008] *Journal of the American Medical Association*. Several study authors, including Ressler, reported having financial ties to makers of psychiatric drugs.

New genetic research has shown that a stress-related gene may play a role in post-traumatic stress disorder. (Andrew Brookes, National Physical Laboratory/ Photo Researchers, Inc.)

Testing for Those at Risk

Ressler noted that there are probably many other gene variants that contribute to risks for PTSD, and others may be more strongly linked to the disorder than the ones the researchers focused on. Still, he and outside experts said the study is important and that similar advances could lead to tests that will help identify who's most at risk. Treatments including psychotherapy and psychiatric drugs could be targeted to those people, Ressler said.

About a quarter of a million Americans will develop PTSD at some point in their lives after being victimized or witnessing violence or other traumatic events. Rates are much higher in war veterans and people living in high-crime areas.

Symptoms can develop long after the event and usually include recurrent terrifying recollections of the trauma. Sufferers often have debilitating anxiety, irritability, insomnia and other signs of stress.

Dr. Thomas Insel, director of the National Institute of Mental Health, said the study is particularly valuable for the light it sheds on military veterans, who are known to be vulnerable to PTSD. He said the results help explain differences in how two people see the same roadside bomb blast. One simply experiences it as "a bad day but goes back and is able to function." The other later develops paralyzing stress symptoms. "This could be quite a wave that will hit us over the months and years ahead," Insel said. His agency paid for the study.

Study participants were mostly low-income black adults, aged 40 on average, who sought non-psychiatric health care at a public hospital in Atlanta. They were asked about experiences in childhood and as adults and gave saliva samples that underwent genetic testing.

Childhood Abuse Victims

Almost 30 percent of participants reported having been sexually or physically abused as children. Most also had experienced trauma as adults, including rape, attacks with weapons and other violence.

Researchers focused on symptoms of PTSD rather than an actual diagnosis, and found that about 25 percent had stress symptoms severe enough to meet criteria for the disorder, Ressler said.

Childhood abuse and adult trauma each increased risks for PTSD symptoms in adulthood. But the most severe symptoms occurred in the 30 percent of child abuse survivors who had variations in the stress gene.

> **FAST FACT**
>
> In a study of twelve multigenerational families that had experienced a massive earthquake, University of California at Los Angeles researchers found 41 percent of PTSD symptoms were due to genetics.

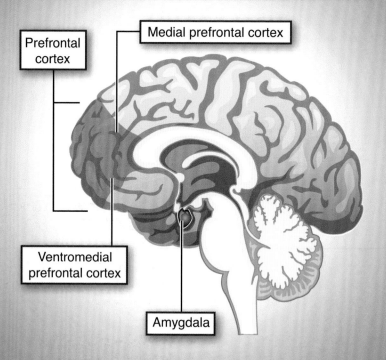

Brain Structures Involved in Dealing with Fear and Stress

Prefrontal cortex

Medial prefrontal cortex

Ventromedial prefrontal cortex

Amygdala

Taken from: www.nimh.nih.gov/health/publications/post-traumatic-stress-disorder-research-fact-sheet/
post-traumatic-stress-disorder-research-fact-sheet.pdf.

Researchers were not able to determine if the symptoms were reactions to the child abuse or to the more recent trauma—or both, said co-author Rebekah Bradley, also of Emory University.

The study is an important contribution to a growing body of research showing how severe abuse early in life can have profound, lasting effects, said Duke University psychiatry expert John Fairbank, co-director of the National Center for Child Traumatic Stress. He was not involved in the research.

CHAPTER 2

The Controversial Side of PTSD

A Broad PTSD Definition May Lead to Overdiagnosis

Scott Allen

With thousands of Iraq War veterans being diagnosed with and treated for PTSD, the issue of correct diagnosis is at the forefront of many medical debates. In the following viewpoint reporter Scott Allen discusses a study done by McLean Hospital in Massachusetts stating that the current definition of PTSD, written in 1994, is outdated and no longer relevant. Allen says that medical science has advanced greatly on this issue in the last decade and a half, and questions are now arising regarding the validity of the definition. Science has shown that PTSD is more closely related to other types of mental illness than was thought when the official definition was written, says Allen. He reports that scientists are now considering the view that a major traumatic event may worsen an existing illness and not necessarily cause PTSD.

Allen is an investigative reporter for *The Boston Globe* with a background in health and science issues.

Photo on previous page. David McBee, an Iraq War veteran, had to endure homelessness while waiting to be treated for PTSD. The treatment of PTSD-afflicted war veterans is highly controversial. (AP Images)

SOURCE: Scott Allen, "Tighter Definition of Post-Traumatic Stress Disorder Needed, Study Says: Research Suggests Diagnoses Inflated," *Boston Globe,* March 21, 2007. Copyright © 2007 Globe Newspaper Company. Reproduced by permission.

The symptoms of post-traumatic stress disorder are so common that depressed people who have never faced trauma usually qualify for the condition, according to a new study that raises questions about whether thousands of Iraq war veterans as well as civilians are getting the right diagnosis and treatment for their emotional problems.

Military researchers estimate that 12 to 20 percent of Iraq war veterans show signs of post-traumatic stress, such as recurrent nightmares, emotional numbness, and high anxiety, and the disorder accounts for half of all mental health disability claims.

Number of PTSD Sufferers Inflated

But the new study by McLean Hospital researchers suggests those numbers may be greatly inflated: Researchers found that almost 80 percent of the depressed people they interviewed showed symptoms of post-traumatic stress even if they could not name a single trauma that could have caused them.

"If you can identify a nasty event which occurred before these symptoms emerged, you can call it post-traumatic stress disorder," said Dr. J. Alexander Bodkin, lead author of the study in [the March 21, 2007] *Journal of Anxiety Disorders*. "I'm not saying there is no such thing as a mood or anxiety disorder caused by traumatic events, but the symptoms [used to classify the illness] are really grossly inadequate."

Correct Diagnosis Is Critical

Bodkin said it's crucial to get the diagnosis right. Though people diagnosed with post-traumatic stress commonly are also treated for depression or anxiety, he said some treatments for post-traumatic stress, such as focusing on "facing" the trauma, could be counterproductive. "It might be worse than a waste of time. Maybe you don't need to work through what is bothering you. Maybe you need to get over what is bothering you," said Bodkin.

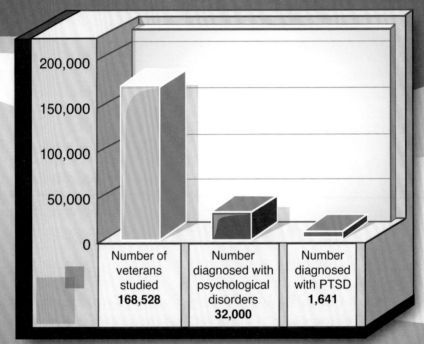

U.S. Veterans of the Iraq War Diagnosed with PTSD

According to a 2005 study by the U.S. Department of Veterans Affairs, a number of Iraq War veterans experience PTSD.

| | Number of veterans studied 168,528 | Number diagnosed with psychological disorders 32,000 | Number diagnosed with PTSD 1,641 |

Taken from: Jack Epstein and Johnny Miller, "U.S. Wars and Post-Traumatic Stress Disorder," *San Francisco Chronicle*, June 22, 2005. www.sfgate.com.

The study joins a growing body of research that questions whether post-traumatic stress disorder is a distinct mental illness, at least as it is currently defined. Unlike other mental illnesses, the diagnosis of post-traumatic stress disorder begins not with the patient's symptoms, but with identifying a major trauma such as witnessing a murder or fighting in a war. Critics say that can lead therapists to falsely conclude that the symptoms were caused by the trauma. It could be that the trauma worsened an underlying condition such as depression or anxiety.

Changing the Definition of PTSD

[On March 20, 2007], psychiatric researchers who wrote the post-traumatic stress disorder definition agreed that the definition needs to be tightened. Psychologist David Barlow of Boston University said the official definition, which he helped develop in 1994, has become outdated as advances in brain science suggest that post-traumatic stress is more closely related to other conditions than researchers recognized at the time.

Psychologist David Barlow, who helped develop the definition of PTSD in 1994, now believes advances in brain science call for a re-evaluation of PTSD symptoms. (AP Images)

"We might need to step back a level and begin looking at what these disorders have in common," said Barlow, then cochairman of the committee that wrote the post-traumatic stress disorder section for the psychiatrists' bible, the *Diagnostic and Statistical Manual of Mental Disorders*, or *DSM*.

PTSD Diagnosis Is Overused

However, Dr. Michael First, editor of the *DSM*, said he believes post-traumatic stress disorder is a separate disorder. "My concern is that it's overused," said First, of Columbia University. "It started out as combat neuroses for very severely traumatized soldiers, but now it's all over the place."

> **FAST FACT**
>
> Nearly 12 percent of active duty soldiers who have been deployed in Iraq or Afganistan have served three or more tours of duty in those locations.

Post-traumatic stress disorder wasn't officially recognized as a mental illness until 1980, as a growing number of Vietnam combat veterans complained of flashbacks, nightmares, and other symptoms that their doctors said were rooted in the horrors that they had witnessed. With the inclusion of post-traumatic stress disorder in the *DSM*, veterans whose symptoms didn't match any existing disease would become eligible for treatment and, potentially, disability benefits, while civilians would become eligible for private insurance coverage.

Some 5.2 million US adults suffer from post-traumatic stress disorder each year, according to the National Center for PTSD, but the risk is highest among military personnel. [In 2006], the Department of Veterans Affairs granted 269,399 claims for disability based on post-traumatic stress, accounting for 48.9 percent of all mental health disability claims.

Is Trauma the Cause of Mental Illness?

But skeptics questioned whether one trauma, even one as horrific as war, could be the root of so much mental illness; more likely, they argued that stress worsens underlying conditions and that, for some, even a minor trauma could act as a trigger. For instance, one study showed that college students who had suffered only minor traumas, such as getting stuck in an elevator, were more likely to show PTSD symptoms than those who had suffered major loss.

The researchers at McLean Hospital interviewed 103 depression patients using the same survey that a counselor would to diagnose post-traumatic stress. If patients hadn't suffered a serious loss, they were urged to discuss even a minor trauma that caused them recurrent distress. Researchers found that 79 percent had PTSD symptoms, including 28 patients who could not come up with one traumatic memory.

Bodkin said the results show that the definition of post-traumatic stress disorder is unreliable. "People have just been averting their eyes since 1980 from some pretty glaring scientific problems," he said.

PTSD Is Not Overdiagnosed

Alain Brunet, Vivian Akerib, and Philippe Birmes

According to the authors of the following viewpoint, PTSD did not increase dramatically as expected after the September 11, 2001, terrorist attacks in New York, Washington, D.C., and Pennsylvania. The authors state that the criteria for diagnosing PTSD have undergone several changes in the last two decades, including improvements in defining, detecting, and assessing traumatic events and their aftermath, in order to more accurately categorize the disorder. The authors also believe that PTSD is underdiagnosed in several subgroups such as men and young children.

Alain Brunet is an assistant professor at McGill University and a researcher at Douglas Hospital Research Center, both in Montreal; Vivian Akerib is a psychologist with the Douglas Hospital Research Center; and Philippe Birmes is a professor in the Department of Psychology at the University of Toulouse in France.

SOURCE: Alain Brunet, Vivian Akerib, and Philippe Birmes, "Don't Throw Out the Baby with the Bathwater (PTSD Is Not Overdiagnosed)," *Canadian Journal of Psychiatry*, August, 2007. Reproduced by permission.

In the aftermath of the terrorist attacks on the World Trade Center, some media "experts" predicted that up to 1 out of 5 New Yorkers would suffer from full-blown posttraumatic stress disorder (PTSD). In fact, 2 months after the attacks, among a random sample of 1008 adults living in Manhattan, only 7.5% reported symptoms consistent with a diagnosis of acute PTSD. It is relatively easy these days to find instances among the media and the general public where the concept of psychological trauma is overapplied or misrepresented, giving the impression that PTSD must be rampant and therefore overdiagnosed. Despite the popular use of this term, actual prevalence rates demonstrate that PTSD is not overdiagnosed by those whose job it is to diagnose: the epidemiologists [doctors who study the spread of disease] and the mental health professionals. If we consider the evolution in the field of trauma research, there are at least 2 major tendencies: on the one hand, the criteria for diagnosing PTSD have become stricter, while, on the other hand, our ability to detect and correctly assess trauma exposure and PTSD has improved, thereby leading to the identification of new, previously undiagnosed cases. The net result of these 2 tendencies is a remarkably stable rate of PTSD in the epidemiologic surveys of the last decade.

Changes in the Diagnostic Criteria of PTSD

The diagnostic criteria of PTSD have undergone many minor changes since they were introduced in the *DSM-III* [*Diagnostic and Statistical Manual of Mental Disorders,* third edition] (1980). With the publication of *DSM-IV* (1994), however, a major change was introduced: the definition of what constitutes a traumatic event shifted from a nomothetic [generalized] to an idiographic [unique to an individual] one. From that point on, trauma was no longer defined as an objective event but rather as a life-threatening experience that must, in addition, be appraised by the exposed individual with fear, helplessness, or horror. In the absence of such distress, the event was no longer considered traumatic. In many instances, this change dramatically reduced the number of individuals typically considered as having been exposed to a traumatic event. In addition, the emergence of the social impairment criterion in the *DSM-IV* (for all mental disorders) decreased the prevalence rate of PTSD up to 24%, according to a recent study.

Changes in Epidemiologic Survey Methodology

Although the criteria for diagnosing PTSD have evolved toward being more restrictive, our ability to detect and assess trauma has also improved. For instance, in epidemiologic surveys, lists of potentially qualifying events (and the use of explicit definitions, as in the case of sexual abuse) to prime the memory of the participants are now routinely used, something which was not done in the earlier surveys. As a result of this and other methodological improvements, the rates of PTSD did go up. For instance, in 1987 [J.E.] Helzer et al found in the Epidemiological Catchment Area study a lifetime rate of PTSD of only 1%. Since then, however, large surveys conducted in the United States have found higher but remarkably similar rates of lifetime PTSD: 7.5% and 6.6% in 2 representative samples of the US population and a conditional risk of 9.1% among the exposed in a sample of young urban US adults. This stabilization of the PTSD rate in carefully designed epidemiologic surveys argues strongly against the idea that PTSD is overdiagnosed. . . .

PTSD and the Issue of Comorbidity

The early epidemiologic studies illustrate how easy it is to miss a diagnosis of PTSD if one does not have the right investigative tools. There are several other reasons why it remains easy to miss a diagnosis of PTSD. One of them is comorbidity [accompanying but unrelated disease pro-

A study of U.S. soldiers who served in Operation Iraqi Freedom from December 2005 to November 2006 revealed a variety of mental health problems—both in those serving for the first time and in those who had had multiple deployments.

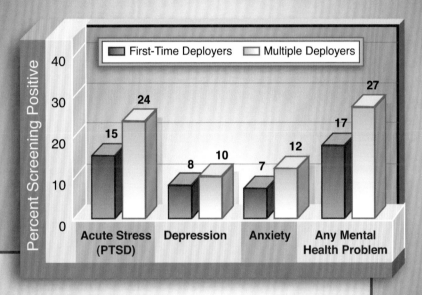

Taken from: Office of the Surgeon General U.S. Army Medical Command, "Mental Health Advisory Team (MHAT) IV Operation Iraqi Freedom 05–07."

cess]; 84% of individuals with PTSD meet criteria for at least one other psychiatric disorder. Comorbid disorders such as major depression, alcohol abuse, substance abuse, specific phobias, panic disorder, schizophrenia, and anti-social and borderline personality disorder may all be di-agnosed first, thereby relegating the individual's trauma history (and possible PTSD) to the background. In fact, now that PTSD is an established disorder, the contribu-tion of trauma exposure to the development of mental health problems other than PTSD is beginning to receive more attention. PTSD may similarly be underdiagnosed in individuals suffering from medical conditions such as traumatic brain injury, cancer, chronic pain, fibromyalgia, and paralysis. Greater awareness with respect to the diagnosis of PTSD has led, and will in the future lead, to the detection of cases that were previously going unnoticed.

PTSD Remains Underdiagnosed in Several Subgroups

PTSD is still underdiagnosed in several important subgroups. In Western countries, it is well known that men tend to underreport psychiatric symptoms, relative to women. Likewise, cases have been reported of intake interviews of young children resulting in no diagnosis of PTSD

Battered women with PTSD are often underdiagnosed as a group because they rarely come to the attention of mental health professionals. (© Janine Wiedel Photolibrary/Alamy)

unless corroborating evidence was taken from parents or other adults. Street prostitutes, who typically report high rates of lifetime trauma exposure and PTSD, rarely come to the attention of mental health professionals, and may not be included in epidemiologic surveys. Other such examples include battered women in shelters, immigrants coming from countries with oppressive regimes, First Nations people [original inhabitants of Canada] living on Reserves, the homeless, and prison inmates. Cultural norms may also in some instances restrict diagnosis. For example, in Asians the symptoms of PTSD are primarily expressed as somatization [converting mental experiences into physical symptoms], and patients will often present to their general practitioner with physical complaints.

> **FAST FACT**
>
> A 2007 study of one hundred thousand veterans seen at VA health care facilities found that 56 percent had two or more mental health diagnoses.

The Issue of Malingering

In closing, a word needs to be said about malingering [intentionally faking or exaggerating physical symptoms or ailments for personal gain]. All mental disorders are prone to malingering when there are secondary gains, and PTSD is no exception. However, in the case of PTSD, the reverse is also true. Stigma is perhaps most prevalent in the very occupations where PTSD is most likely, such as among law enforcement and corrections officers, emergency workers, firefighters, and soldiers. In many societies, there is also limited support for reporting crime-related trauma or "shameful" sexual trauma, which carry another form of stigma.

Increased Awareness of PTSD Is Beneficial

In summary, we have argued that the official diagnostic criteria for PTSD have, in fact, become stricter over the last 25 years; that the moderate increase in the rate of PTSD cases observed in the late 1990s most likely reflects our improved capacity to detect trauma and our increasing awareness of the role played by trauma in the etiology of mental health problems, rather than a pandemic of new PTSD cases; that several subgroups exist whose PTSD is still underrecognized; and that prevailing social stigma probably still leads to the underestimation of the true rate of PTSD in our societies.

Although frivolous claims of PTSD will likely continue to occur from time to time, the public debate and increased awareness about the hidden human and financial costs of traumatogenic events such as warfare, rape, and child abuse—to name just a few—must continue for the good of society. From a scientific perspective, PTSD probably represents one of the best models in psychiatry of a gene x environment interaction. Does this renewed interest for the role of trauma exposure in the etiology of mental disorders represent the advent of a truly biopsychosocial psychiatry? Time will tell.

The Debriefing Debate

National Center for Posttraumatic Stress Disorder

One of the methods used to treat PTSD patients is debriefing. This technique requires a counselor to help a patient relive the details of the traumatic event in the hope that it will lessen its impact. Three different types of debriefing counseling can be utilized under specific circumstances. According to the National Center for Posttraumatic Stress Disorder, part of the Department of Veterans Affairs, recent research has shown that debriefing is not always the best way to treat someone following a traumatic event. A review of eight different debriefing studies has shown that in some instances debriefing can actually increase the incidence of traumatic stress. Another concern with debriefing regards the experience of the person doing the counseling. In group sessions it is often difficult for the counselor to sufficiently assess the extent of the distress that an individual is experiencing. Debriefing is most effective when conducted by experienced practitioners.

The National Center for Posttraumatic Stress Disorder provides research and education on the prevention and treatment of PTSD.

SOURCE: "Types of Debriefing Following Disasters," National Center for Posttraumatic Stress Disorder, 2008. Reproduced by permission.

The aim of all disaster mental-health management, including any type of debriefing, should be the humane, competent, and compassionate care of all affected. The goal should be to prevent adverse health outcomes and to enhance the well-being of individuals and communities. In particular, it is vital to use all appropriate endeavors to prevent the development of chronic and disabling problems such as PTSD, depression, alcohol abuse, and relationship difficulties. Debriefings are a type of intervention that are sometimes used following a disaster or other traumatic event.

Different Types of Debriefing

- Operational debriefing is a routine and formal part of an organizational response to a disaster. Mental-health workers acknowledge it as an appropriate practice that may help survivors acquire an overall sense of meaning and a degree of closure.
- Psychological or stress debriefing refers to a variety of practices for which there is little supportive empirical evidence. It is strongly suggested that psychological debriefing is not an appropriate mental-health intervention.
- Critical Incident Stress Debriefing (CISD) is a formalized, structured method whereby a group of rescue and response workers reviews the stressful experience of a disaster. CISD was developed to assist first responders such as fire and police personnel; it was not meant for the survivors of a disaster or their relatives. CISD was never intended as a substitute for therapy. It was designed to be delivered in a group format and meant to be incorporated into a larger, multi-component crisis intervention system labeled *Critical Incident Stress Management (CISM)*. CISM includes the following components: pre-crisis intervention; disaster or large-scale demobilization and informational briefings (town meetings); staff advisement; defusing; CISD; one-on-

The Benefits of Psychological Debriefing

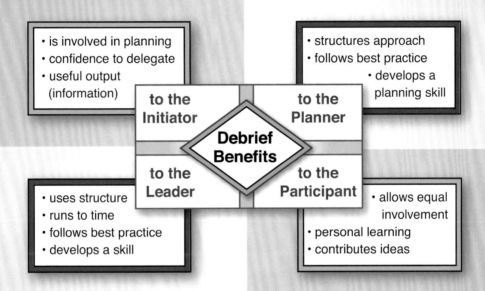

to the Initiator
- is involved in planning
- confidence to delegate
- useful output (information)

to the Planner
- structures approach
- follows best practice
- develops a planning skill

Debrief Benefits

to the Leader
- uses structure
- runs to time
- follows best practice
- develops a skill

to the Participant
- allows equal involvement
- personal learning
- contributes ideas

Taken from: The Centre for Structures Debriefing Ltd., Fleet, Hampshire, England. www.structured-debriefing.co.uk/2structures_debriefing.htm.

one crisis counseling or support; family crisis intervention and organizational consultation; follow-up and referral mechanisms for assessment and treatment, if necessary.

Debriefing Not Always Appropriate

Currently, many mental-health workers consider some form of stress debriefing the standard of care following both natural (earthquakes) and human-caused (workplace shootings, bombings) stressful events. Indeed, the National Center for PTSD's *Disaster Mental Health Guidebook* (which is currently being revised) contains information on how to conduct debriefings. However, recent research indicates that psychological debriefing is not always an appropriate mental-health intervention.

Recent research indicates that psychological debriefing is not appropriate treatment for acutely bereaved individuals. (AP Images)

Available evidence shows that, in some instances, it may increase traumatic stress or complicate recovery. Psychological debriefing is also inappropriate for acutely bereaved individuals. While operational debriefing is nearly always helpful (it involves clarifying events and providing education about normal responses and coping mechanisms), care must be taken before delivering more emotionally focused interventions.

Studies Show No PTSD Reduction

A recent review of eight debriefing studies, all of which met rigorous criteria for being well-controlled, revealed no evidence that debriefing reduces the risk of PTSD, depression, or anxiety; nor were there any reductions in psychiatric symptoms across studies. Additionally, in two studies, one of which included long-term follow-up, some negative effects of CISD-type debriefings were reported relating to PTSD and other trauma-related symptoms. Therefore, debriefings as currently employed may be useful for low magnitude stress exposure and symptoms or for emergency care providers. However, the best studies suggest that for individuals with more severe exposure to trauma, and for those who are experiencing more severe reactions such as PTSD, debriefing is ineffective and possibly harmful.

Reasons for Negative Debriefing Results

The question of why debriefing may produce negative results has been considered and hypotheses have been formulated. One theory connects negative outcomes with heightened arousal in the early posttrauma phase and in long-term psychopathology. Because verbalization of the trauma in debriefing is limited, habituation to evoked distress does not occur. The result may be an increase rather than a decrease in arousal. Any such increased distress caused by debriefing may be difficult to detect in a group setting. Thus, attempting to use debriefing to override dissociation and avoidance in the immediate posttrauma phase may be detrimental to some individuals, particularly those experiencing heightened arousal. Another consideration is that the boundary between debriefing and therapy is sometimes blurred (e.g., challenging thoughts), which may increase distress in some individuals. Finally, those facilitating the debriefing sessions frequently are unable to adequately assess individuals in the group setting. They may erroneously conclude that a one-time intervention is sufficient to prevent further symptomatology.

> **FAST FACT**
>
> Critical incident debriefing was originally developed to help emergency workers cope with traumatic stress as part of their job.

When Debriefing Helps

Practice guidelines on debriefing formulated by the International Society for Traumatic Stress Studies conclude there is little evidence that debriefing prevents psychopathology. The guidelines do recognize that debriefing is often well received and that it may help (1) facilitate the screening of those at risk, (2) disseminate education and referral information, and (3) improve organizational morale. However, the practice guidelines specify that if debriefing is employed, it should:

- Be conducted by experienced, well-trained practitioners
- Not be mandatory
- Utilize some clinical assessment of potential participants
- Be accompanied by clear and objective evaluation procedures

The guidelines state that while it is premature to conclude that debriefing should be discontinued altogether, "more complex interventions for those individuals at highest risk may be the best way to prevent the development of PTSD following trauma."

Propranolol May Not Be Effective Enough in Treating PTSD

Barbara Melville

Propranolol is a drug routinely used to treat high blood pressure. In a study conducted on emergency room patients who had received propranolol after experiencing a traumatic event, propranolol or a placebo was administered four times a day for ten days. In the following viewpoint Barbara Melville discusses the study results and concludes that propranolol did not make a large difference when compared to the placebo. Melville also discusses the ethical concerns regarding this medication, including prescribing it for less critical or trivial purposes and the exploitation of the drug by pharmaceutical companies to make money from peoples' bad memories.

Barbara Melville is a science writer with a background in human biology, neurochemistry, and evolutionary biology.

Propranolol (brand name "Inderel") is a cheap, effective beta blocker used to treat heart problems and anxiety. It is also thought to prevent the onset of post-traumatic stress, when given after traumatic events. This may seem like a promising find; however, many have expressed strong ethical concerns.

What Is Post-Traumatic Stress Disorder?

Post-traumatic stress disorder (PTSD) occurs following frightening or distressing events. It is both physical and psychological, with symptoms usually appearing immediately after or within three months of the event. Symptoms include nightmares, flashbacks, feelings of isolation and feelings of detachment. These symptoms can be lasting and pervasive, significantly affecting the sufferer's quality of life. Sufferers may feel as though they are reliving the event over and over.

Propranolol and Post-Traumatic Stress

Propranolol blocks adrenaline, the hormone that surges when people are shocked or frightened. According to *BMJ Best Treatments*, researchers hypothesized that this action may affect the part of the brain that consolidates emotional memory. The term "amnesia drug" has been used to describe propranolol but is in truth a misnomer, as the drug is not thought to make people literally forget. Instead, it is thought to weaken the emotions attached to memories.

Propranolol and PTSD Research

There is currently little research on this use of propranolol so it is difficult to ascertain if it is truly effective, and why.

A small pilot study published in *Biological Psychiatry* in 2002 suggested that propranolol, administered following trauma, may be effective in preventing PTSD. Subjects of this double-blind trial began treatment within six hours of experiencing trauma, and were administered either propranolol 40mg or a placebo four times per day for 10 days.

There was little difference between the two groups, with the exception that those on propranolol experienced a drop in body stress response when listening to an account of their trauma. This suggested some effect and that it may be worth studying further.

Some small studies have followed that support propranolol for emotional blunting of memories, including sufferers who have been diagnosed with the disorder for some time. However, further investigations are required to substantially prove and better understand its effects.

Ethical Implications of Propranolol

There are a number of ethical concerns about this use of propranolol. Some researchers are concerned about the possible ill effects of altering memory, particularly as memory is not thoroughly understood. Memories store

The use of the drug propranolol to treat PTSD symptoms has raised ethical concerns about its possible ill effects on the memory. (© Julie Woodhouse f/Alamy)

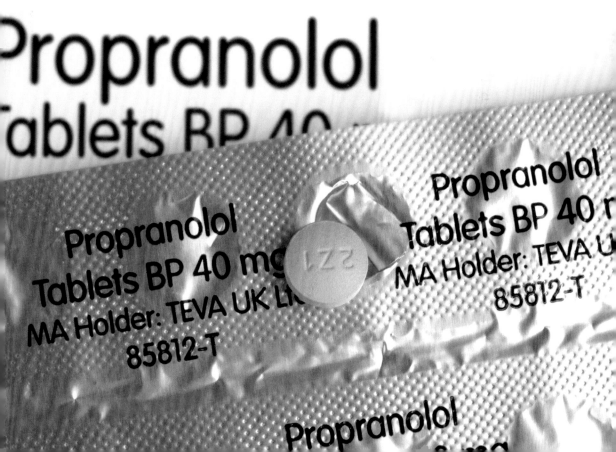

and retrieve information, and undoubtedly they are an important aspect of what make people who they are. One concern is that the drug will be abused for more trivial purposes, such as getting over a bad night out.

An article published in the *American Journal of Bioethics* in 2007 highlighted social concerns regarding this treatment. In particular, if bad memories are pathologized, will the pharmaceutical industry then exploit this for lucrative purposes? They suggest further studies be carried out to ascertain the efficacy of propranolol for preventing PTSD, including investigating the possible ill-effects of diminishing memory.

Some researchers in favor of exploring this drug tend to argue that PTSD should be given the same attention as physical injuries. Some also argue that there are other psychoactive drugs available that change people, and that propranolol's use for PTSD isn't really any different. Although the positive effects of propranolol appear to be a promising possibility for the treatment of PTSD, further investigation is required to explore the related medical ethics.

Propranolol May Be Helpful in Treating PTSD

Associated Press

The following viewpoint explains that the hypertension drug propano-lol is now being tested on individuals who experience post-traumatic stress disorder to help make their traumatic memories less intense and less meaningful or painful. Scientists are also looking at using propranolol as a cure for PTSD by invoking older painful memories and using the drug to get rid of or lessen them. Also discussed in this selection is the finding that traumatic memories stay sharper and more focused in the brain than other memories, and scientists are now using propranolol to lessen the impact of these events.

The Associated Press is one of the largest news organizations providing print, photos, graphics, audio, and video.

Suppose you could erase bad memories from your mind. Suppose, as in a recent movie, your brain could be wiped clean of sad and traumatic thoughts.

That is science fiction. But real-world scientists are working on the next best thing. They have been testing a

SOURCE: "Doctors Test a Drug to Ease Traumatic Memories," msnbc.com, January 15, 2006. © 2008 The Associated Press. Republished with permission.

pill that, when given after a traumatic event like rape, may make the resulting memories less painful and intense.

Will it work? It is too soon to say. Still, it is not far-fetched to think that this drug someday might be passed out along with blankets and food at emergency shelters after disasters like the tsunami or Hurricane Katrina.

Psychiatrist Hilary Klein could have offered it to the man she treated at a St. Louis shelter over the Labor Day weekend. He had fled New Orleans and was so distraught over not knowing where his sisters were that others had to tell Klein his story. "This man could not even give his name, he was in such distress. All he could do was cry," she said.

Such people often develop post-traumatic stress disorder, or PTSD, a problem first recognized in Vietnam War veterans. Only 14 percent to 24 percent of trauma

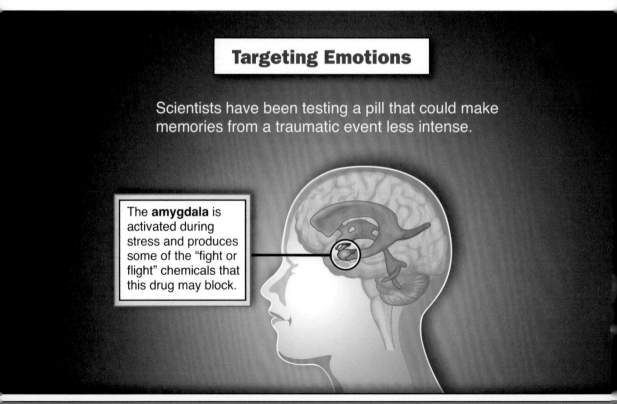

Targeting Emotions

Scientists have been testing a pill that could make memories from a traumatic event less intense.

The **amygdala** is activated during stress and produces some of the "fight or flight" chemicals that this drug may block.

Taken from: Associated Press, "Could a Pill Help Fade Traumatic Memories?" January 15, 2006.

victims experience long-term PTSD, but sufferers have flashbacks and physical symptoms that make them feel as if they are reliving the trauma years after it occurred.

Scientists think it happens because the brain goes haywire during and right after a strongly emotional event, pouring out stress hormones that help store these memories in a different way than normal ones are preserved. Taking a drug to tamp down these chemicals might blunt memory formation and prevent PTSD, they theorize.

Some doctors have an even more ambitious goal: trying to cure PTSD. They are deliberately triggering very old bad memories and then giving the pill to deep-six them.

The first study to test this approach on 19 longtime PTSD sufferers has provided early encouraging results, Canadian and Harvard University researchers report. "We figure we need to test about 10 more people until we've got solid evidence," said Alain Brunet, a psychologist at McGill University in Montreal who is leading the study.

It can't come too soon.

Shapable Memories

The need for better treatment grows daily as American troops return from Iraq and Afghanistan with wounded minds as well as bodies. One government survey found almost 1 in 6 showing symptoms of mental stress, including many with post-traumatic stress disorder. Disability payments related to the illness cost the government more than $4 billion a year.

The need is even greater in countries ravaged by many years of violence.

"I don't think there's yet in our country a sense of urgency about post-traumatic stress disorder" but there should be, said James McGaugh, director of the Center for the Neurobiology of Learning and Memory at the University of California at Irvine. He and a colleague, Larry Cahill, did experiments that changed how scientists view memory formation and suggested new ways to modify it.

Memories, painful or sweet, don't form instantly after an event but congeal over time. Like slowly hardening cement, there is a window of opportunity when they are shapable. During stress, the body pours out adrenaline and other "fight or flight" hormones that help write memories into the "hard drive" of the brain, McGaugh and Cahill showed.

Blunting the Trauma

Propranolol can blunt this. It is in a class of drugs called beta blockers and is the one most able to cross the blood-brain barrier and get to where stress hormones are wreaking havoc. It already is widely used to treat high blood pressure and is being tested for stage fright.

Dr. Roger Pitman, a Harvard University psychiatrist, did a pilot study to see whether it could prevent symptoms of PTSD. He gave 10 days of either the drug or dummy pills to accident and rape victims who came to the Massachusetts General Hospital emergency room.

In follow-up visits three months later, the patients listened to tapes describing their traumatic events as researchers measured their heart rates, palm sweating and forehead muscle tension. The eight who had taken propranolol had fewer stress symptoms than the 14 who received dummy pills, but the differences in the frequency of symptoms were so small they might have occurred by chance—a problem with such tiny experiments. Still, "this was the first study to show that PTSD could be prevented," McGaugh said, and enough to convince the federal government to fund a larger one that Pitman is doing now.

Meanwhile, another study on assault and accident victims in France confirmed that propranolol might prevent PTSD symptoms.

Painful Memory Does Not Decay

One of those researchers, Brunet, now has teamed with Pitman on the boldest experiment yet—trying to cure

longtime PTSD sufferers. "We are trying to reopen the window of opportunity to modulate the traumatic memory," Pitman said.

The experiments are being done in Montreal and involve people traumatized as long as 20 or 30 years ago by child abuse, sexual assault or a serious accident.

"It's amazing how a traumatic memory can remain very much alive. It doesn't behave like a regular memory. The memory doesn't decay," Brunet said.

To try to make it decay, researchers ask people to describe the trauma as vividly as they can, bringing on physical symptoms like racing hearts, then give them propranolol to blunt "restorage" of the memory. As much as three months later, the single dose appears to be preventing PTSD symptoms, Brunet said.

Joseph LeDoux, a neuroscience professor at New York University, is enrolling 20 to 30 people in a similar

A light micrograph shows crystals of the drug propranolol. A beta blocker, it has been used in therapy in an effort to block memories of trauma in PTSD patients. **(Sidney Moulds/Photo Researchers, Inc.)**

experiment and believes in the approach. "Each time you retrieve a memory it must be restored," he said. "When you activate a memory in the presence of a drug that prevents the restorage of the memory, the next day the memory is not as accessible."

Part of the Human Experience

Not all share his enthusiasm, as McGaugh found when he was asked to brief the President's Council on Bioethics a few years ago. "They didn't say anything at the time but later they went ballistic on it," he said.

Chairman Leon Kass contended that painful memories serve a purpose and are part of the human experience.

McGaugh says that's preposterous when it comes to trauma like war. If a soldier is physically injured, "you do everything you can to make him whole," but if he says he is upset "they say, 'suck it up—that's the normal thing,'" he complained.

Propranolol couldn't be given to soldiers in battle because it would curb survival instincts. "They need to be able to run and to fight," Pitman said. "But if you could take them behind the lines for a couple of days, then you could give it to them after a traumatic event," or before they're sent home, he said.

Some critics suggest that rape victims would be less able to testify against attackers if their memories were blunted, or at least that defense attorneys would argue that.

"Medical concerns trump legal concerns. I wouldn't withhold an effective treatment from somebody because of the possibility they may have to go to court a year later and their testimony be challenged. We wouldn't do that in any other area of medicine," Pitman said. "The important thing to know about this drug is it doesn't put a hole in their memory. It doesn't create amnesia."

FAST FACT

In 1988 James W. Black was awarded the Nobel Prize in Medicine for his discovery of propranolol in the 1950s.

Reducing or Preventing PTSD

Practical matters may limit propranolol's usefulness. It must be given within a day or two of trauma to prevent PTSD.

How long any benefits from the drug will last is another issue. McGaugh said some animal research suggests that memory eventually recovers after being squelched for a while by the drug.

Overtreatment also is a concern. Because more than three-quarters of trauma victims don't have long-term problems, most don't need medication.

But LeDoux sees little risk in propranolol. "It's a pretty harmless drug," he said. "If you could give them one or two pills that could prevent PTSD, that would be a pretty good thing."

Klein, the Saint Louis University psychiatrist, said it would be great to have something besides sleep aids, antidepressants and counseling to offer traumatized people, but she remains skeptical about how much long-term good propranolol can do. "If there were a pill to reduce the intensity of symptoms, that would be a relief," she said. "But that's a far step from being able to prevent the development of PTSD."

Only more study will tell whether that is truly possible.

CHAPTER 3

The Personal Side of PTSD

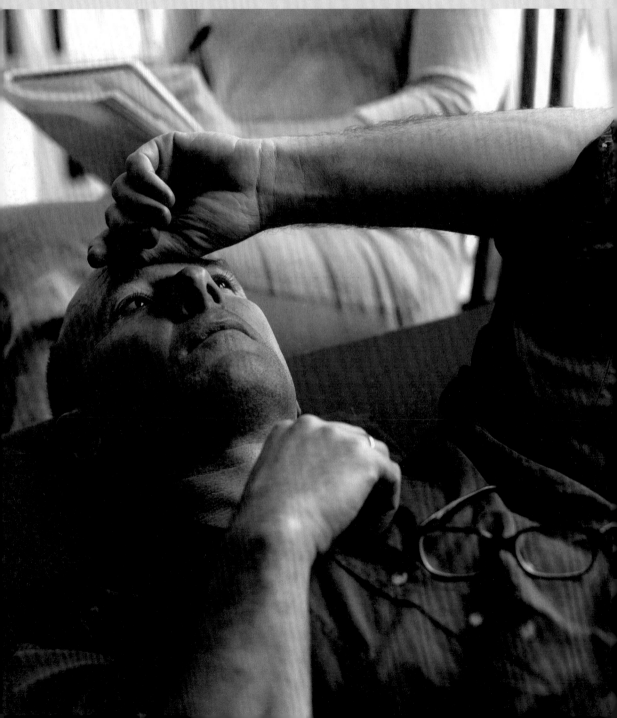

PTSD Following the 2001 World Trade Center Attacks

Leslie Haskin

Leslie Haskin was an employee of Kemper Insurance Company and working on the thirty-sixth floor of the World Trade Center building on the morning of September 11, 2001. In the following excerpt Haskin talks about her post-traumatic stress disorder following the terrorist attacks of that day. She describes her flashbacks, her inability to cross a bridge, her anxiety, and her fear of terrorists being all around her. She also talks about the length of time that PTSD can affect someone and how much progress she has made in creating a normal life for herself.

*J*ournal Entry–October 2001.

She claims she wants me to explain why I wouldn't stay in that psych ward, but I know she knows. . . . I'm not that crazy. GOD!!!!!!!!! Ahhhhhh!!!

I don't know why she keeps asking the same questions . . . told her exactly what I remember happened the day after

SOURCE: Leslie Haskin, *Between Heaven and Ground Zero,* Ada, MI: Bethany House, 2007. Copyright © 2006 by Leslie Haskin. Reproduced by permission.

Photo on facing page. Adult PTSD sufferers have problems with sights and sounds that bring back memories of traumatic events. **(Mauro Fermariello/Photo Researchers, Inc.)**

they tried to kill me . . . somebody drove me to Dr. Rohan's office. I think it was . . . Marcia . . . his assistant was waiting for me outside . . . she grabbed my arm and helped me in. . . . Doctor Rohan took my blood pressure . . . he made a sound like he was dying . . . p.s. everything sounds like it's dying . . . whatever the shot was, made my head hurt worse . . . he explained PTSD, gave me more pills and blah . . . what don't she understand . . . that's all I remember. Period . . . its like I'm still in that fog . . . it still feels like I'm watching it happen . . . God, please . . . please. . . .

If she thinks I'm going back to that hospital, she's got another thing comin'. . . . p.s. Ronnie left yesterday . . . again.

No More Business Decisions

This is my story. I woke up one morning, dressed in business attire, and went to work fully expecting a normal day. Instead, I rode an elevator thirty-six floors and got off in the middle of a lunatic's delusion of justice.

The terrorist attacks of September 11 shattered my life and left me with nothing to rebuild. After years of making carefully planned career decisions, fourteen-hour workdays, hundreds of power suits and power lunches, I couldn't even decide whether to get out of bed or not.

I had flashbacks that caused me to react. They felt as real as being there all over again. I could smell the building. I could hear the bells. I was drawn to roadkill. And no matter where I was when a flashback occurred, my muscles tensed until I was in pain, and my only urge was to make it stop, even if that meant aimlessly running or doing even more unreasonable things like making my friends pull over on high mountain roads.

There were days when I had to sit down in order to feel my legs beneath me, and disturbing uncontrollable trembling forced me behind doors.

Around-the-Clock Anxiety

I was anxious all the time and afraid of my own backyard, convinced that the Taliban was hiding in my shed. I boarded my windows with thick wooden shutters in fear that "they" would get in and murder us all. I put home-made weapons near my bed "just in case" and prayed all night for deliverance.

My future was hopeless. Unable to cross bridges, pass through tunnels, get on elevators, or enter high-rises, I couldn't return to work. I couldn't drive without thinking that trucks alongside me were carrying missiles that would suddenly explode as I passed. I had panic attacks when left alone and anxiety attacks when too many people were around. Sleep was impossible without sleeping pills, which only worked for a few hours.

I would lie awake and watch the sky in fear of what might fall. I walked the floors, jumped at every unfamiliar sound, and feared that sleep would never again be something to long for. There was no end to the constant replays and haunting sounds of what I had lived through.

What was it like? Don't try to imagine that every step you take could be your last. Rather, feel your heart beating your body into an uncontrollable convulsion. What did it look like? The gruesome, the shocking, the reality is that hell must be close. How did it feel? Don't feel. Rather, find yourself in a state of nothingness between a quiet slumber and a ghastly actuality—a "fog" if you will, a nightmare from which you cannot awake.

A Tomb of Despair

Sleep or slumber in a tomb of despair
The eyes of danger watching, there
What price to pay or penalty to keep
For those once calming words . . . "Now I lay me down to
*   sleep"*
Whisper to me . . . or sing me a lullaby
Of winds and of angels and of worlds that don't die
Tell me your secrets, then whisk me away
From the place of disdain in which I now lay
Ever cold, ever deep, ever-hallowed ground . . .
Sleeping here and slumbering there
Forever now—in a tomb of despair.

The Reality of PTSD

PTSD is probably one of the most difficult disorders to describe. It's a very mean disease. It has no friends and makes no excuses. In fact, I don't believe a word exists in the English language that encompasses its whole sphere of related emotions, symptoms, and overall feeling of being "finished."

In the months following the tragedy, reality was still too big for me to wrap my arms around it all. I couldn't face the details, so I withdrew from therapy. I went to the sessions, but that's all.

Doctors suggested it would be years before I would be able to process everything and regain full mental capacity. They even considered the possibility that I might never return to a truly "productive" state of mind.

Days went by before I could leave my home. Weeks passed and I had yet to fully realize the enormity of rubble replacing my towers. I saw more than a fair share of mindless days spent doing absolutely nothing but wishing my misery away.

Months passed before I slept. Years have gone by and some details are still lost. Every now and then old colleagues feed me bits and pieces of what might be buried inside me.

Some have suggested that it was in fact the street-level of the concourse where I was lost and not the plaza. Others remember seeing me picking up body parts rather than stepping over them. Marcia, my neighbor, spoke about me taking a shower and asking for cigarettes, and by the way, she was sixty-one.

Although I have accepted the fact that some details are probably forever lost in the catacombs and grand ruins of what was once my future, I still listen to my friends with an almost unbearable desire to put their pieces together with mine and finally see the big picture.

I have struggled, and as upsetting a reality as it might be, I have considered all of the what-ifs. I realize that

Many survivors of the September 11, 2001, World Trade Center attacks have experienced PTSD symptoms. (**Shannon Stapleton/Reuters/ Landov**)

one pause too many or one step in the wrong direction could have been fatal. What if the airplane had hit the tower lower or just fifteen minutes earlier; if I had left the stairs as the stranger suggested; if the last door had never opened. My story would be one of the unknown. Instead, this is my testimony of God's grace.

Journal Writings

Journal Entry

> I dreamed I was at work, but this time I was carrying a rope. The plane hit the tower as it had before, but instead of going into shock, I walked through the entire

building blowing a horn and telling people to leave. This time I threw a rope from the 99th floor all the way to the ground so that people could slide down to the crowd on the streets. One by one, they went before me and I coordinated the entire thing. I never saw the end of the dream. I woke up in distress, sweating, hyperventilating in a panic and in tears.

Journal Entry

I went into the basement again today. This time I stayed down there longer. I walked all the way to the other side holding my breath and trying to imagine what it's like being buried alive. I closed my eyes, but never got past being alone. I can't imagine what Michael went through. I never got past being alone.

Journal Entry

Ronnie's gonna try to leave again tomorrow. He has to get back to school. I'm so scared I don't know what to do. I can't bear the thought of being alone. Who's gonna protect me and Eliot? Oh God, please help me!!!!!!!!!

The Help of a Pastor

I survived the attack, yes, but there is nothing particularly special about me. I am an everyday kind of woman. The woman you see sitting alone on the park bench—pensive. The one awkwardly smiling as she squeezes into the pew next to you on Sunday morning—late. I am that woman counting in her head and fidgeting with her groceries at checkout—average, normal, everyday. And in my everyday is where God collected all my symptoms and I began to live again.

Pastor John Torres is a lot like my brother Lawrence. He is a very private, calm man with a very deliberate way about him. He doesn't waste words. He says what he means and means what he says in a kind but firm sort of way.

One day, almost a year after the attacks, I sat in his office confused, looking for answers and trying to figure out how to tell him that most nights I still lie awake wanting to tear through my own skin to escape the pain. I spoke softly, stammering, trying to process through the trauma by giving him a minute-by-minute account of what had happened.

He listened for almost an hour, and then interrupted. "You know, Leslie," he said. "It's okay to move slowly through your journey to healing. It's okay to still be disturbed by what you remember and it's even okay not to be okay. God's grace is never ending. His mercies go on for as long as you need them . . . forever."

God's grace and His mercies endure. . . .

And so, I survived, yes, but there is no self-righteousness with me, no delusions of great spiritual discernment. I'm not special, nor do I know the secrets of healing through PTSD beyond what has been revealed through modern medicine.

What I know is that God's grace really is so much more than sufficient and His mercy covers multitudes of pain, providing healing permanence.

And the peace of God . . .

> **FAST FACT**
>
> PTSD specialist Matthew Tull reports that 20 percent of people living below Canal Street (near the World Trade Center) had PTSD following the September 11 terrorist attacks.

God and Gardens

I loved my garden. I enjoyed the texture and natural beauty of flowers and the light fragrance of spring. I'd sit in the middle of my flower beds sometimes and bury my hands in the dirt until I was euphoric. Every year I planted several varieties of flowers. Sometimes I would plant, prune, or weed until the sun went down.

One day I was pruning my roses. I handled them tenderly and with care—to make them beautiful. A thought came to my mind about how God prunes us with the same technique. I smiled at the thought of having Him touch me in any way at all. In fact, I yearned for it.

Then a plane flew overhead. I stopped breathing. Without thinking, I got up and ran down my driveway in a panic . . . going nowhere. I just reacted . . . and ran.

Miraculously, I'm past that now. I stopped running from death and found life in Jesus Christ. I found peace in believing His promise that one day after all is over, I will meet Him in a glorious celebration of overcoming. It's what I live for.

Still Healing from the Trauma

I still wake from time to time to the sickening sound of my own screams. I still grieve the loss of life and for the loved ones left behind. I still pray for the orphaned children and hope for their futures.

As shocking as it might sound, my senses still retain a bit of that day, as my sense of smell is heightened and I will walk aimlessly about a room just to find the remains of a single burned match.

But these things no longer limit my life. My days are filled to capacity with the hope of His glory. And when I feel crisp, subtle winds blowing gently across the night, and the dew tickles my skin with a playful tease—when I see the nearest cloud is a trillion light years away and stars are floating in the sky like diamonds—I smile back at God and I . . . breathe.

The Effects of Vietnam

Maryallyn Fisher, as told to Penny Coleman

Maryallyn Fisher is the widow of a Vietnam veteran. In the following selection Penny Coleman presents Fisher's story in her own words. Fisher talks about what it was like to live with her husband after he returned from the war. She describes the two versions of her husband—"good" Dennis and "bad" Dennis—and how she always took care of everything and made restitution with others when bad Dennis did something wrong. After several years, countless visits to the Department of Veteran Affairs and therapy sessions, and many different medications, PTSD was diagnosed. Fisher also talks about how women's support groups helped her cope with her situation and her shame and, ultimately, her husband's suicide.

Ugly men could not have gotten away with what Dennis got away with. That's the truth—I would never have taken it, none of his women would have, and he had a lot of women. I was Mrs. Fisher the

SOURCE: Penny Coleman, *Flashback: Posttraumatic Stress Disorder, Suicide, and the Lessons of War,* Boston: Beacon Press, 2006. Copyright © 2006 by Penny Coleman. All rights reserved. Reprinted by permission of Beacon Press, Boston.

third. I've never seen such a handsome man in my whole entire life. He used to take my breath away.

The Good and the Bad Dennis

There was never a doubt in my mind that he loved me, but there was the really good Dennis and then there was the really bad Dennis. He would go out on these binges and he would write bad checks. I would say, "Okay, don't worry about the bad checks; I'll go down in the morning and pay for them. Oh, you stole from your mother? I'll go down and deal with your mother and, yes, I'll make sure that she doesn't call the police. Here's something to eat." I mean, I just took care of everything, and nothing I was doing was working. When I took care of all the problems for him, that didn't work. When I threw him out, that didn't work. Screaming and going to therapy, that didn't work. When I let him take the medication in the house, that didn't work; he just abused the medication. Nothing I was doing was working, but I didn't think it was his destiny to die. I thought that God had a different plan or he would've been dead a long time ago. Dennis was a dope fiend. You don't use dope the way Dennis used dope and stay alive, so I always thought that he was going to stop, that he was going to get clean. I just believed that in my heart, that it wasn't his destiny; that it wasn't our daughter Jean-Marie's or my destiny either. I didn't know what it was going to take, but something was going to have to happen, and then he was doing better and we were going to be okay.

The Everyday Issues

So what was he doing? Drinking. He worked as a carpenter, and at an oil refinery, but those were short stretches, like two-three months. He was never able to hold a long-term job. Authority issues, for sure. And his anxiety level was too high. He would go into rages over nothing. He wouldn't sleep for like three days, and then he would be crazy. The holidays were a nightmare; planes, helicopters, everything was a nightmare. He couldn't handle anything. I didn't know what his problem was, but I wanted that shit to stop. I was the one that was starting to lose it, because he was doing weird stuff that nobody else would understand. Nobody else does understand unless they're married to a PTSD vet.

Vietnam Experiences

Dennis didn't talk about Vietnam at all, so I don't know all the details. But I know he got blown up over in Vietnam. He was in something like a tank, and there were, I think, six of them, and a hand grenade flew in there. They all died except for Dennis. I know that that was one of the traumas. There was a little girl that he befriended that one of the officers raped, and that upset him. Also, he was in a helicopter, and the guy who had the machine gun got shot to death, and Dennis had to move him and take over the machine gun. Shrapnel went through his shoulder and through his neck, about an inch away from the base of his spine. His disability was 110 percent. They only gave him 10 percent for the PTSD.

PTSD Reality

We didn't even talk about PTSD until we had been married for a few years, Jean-Marie had been born; and he was in therapy. He'd been living with symptoms for years, but nobody knew what it was. A diagnosis of post-traumatic stress? From the V.A. [Department of Veteran Affairs]? Forget it! We had to fight for that. This was the '80s and nobody I talked to had any understanding of PTSD. They just wanted to get him out. They came to my house every night with a big padded envelope of medications, all types: Vicodin, Methodone cocktail, Paxil. Take this, go away. Towards the end when he got really bad, he would go to bed in November and wouldn't get out of bed until March. And that's the truth.

It was a big thing in therapy when we finally understood that it was PSTD. It took six months, just working on that one thing. He would be screaming and telling me it was all me, and I would say, "Dennis it's your PTSD," and instead of saying, "No it's not, you f--- bitch, it's you!" he would finally say, "Okay, I'll think about that," and he would go out to the garage and do it. We had gotten to that point, but he just couldn't go through to the other side. He'd have to hit the bar.

I gave up the last two years. Actually, I should have left two or three years before I did. Nothing was working. He didn't need to go out and drink, he didn't need to do cocaine. We had a whole cabinet filled with different types of medication from the V.A. He just started abusing the medication like he did the other drugs.

The Help of Support Groups

There were some good people running the support groups at the Vet Center in Bellingham, Washington. I was going to the Partners of Vets with PTSD. I had been in groups before with women who were exactly like me—they couldn't get out either. I would listen to them talk about their lives and think, "Are you out of your mind? You're crazy!" Then I'd look around, and I'm in the circle with them. That's when I really felt isolated, because I wasn't going anywhere. But the women's group at the Bellingham center helped me tremendously. These women got it, and they helped me decide that I would not go into my forties being this crazy. And it was that crazy. Jean-Marie was cutting herself because she was that messed up. There was no way I could keep her there. I turned forty in September, stalled until February, and then put everything I could into the car and grabbed the kid. Certain things I couldn't take, like my jewelry box that had my charm bracelet in it, charms my parents had given me. I couldn't take them because if I took them it meant I wasn't coming back.

Suicide

I had been gone a year and a half when I got the phone call. It was the Everson police, and I thought, okay, now what did he do? But the cop said Dennis had shot himself. I wouldn't let them take him off the life support until we got there. Because if only his heart was beating, I had to get there before. I kept calling the hospital, saying keep him going until—just don't let his heart stop until we get there.

They had a white cloth over him and his eyes were open and I could see his green eyes. He was still warm and his heart was still beating. I was there when his heart went down from 64 to 32 to 19 to 6 to 2. I had my arms around him, I had my head on his chest, and I heard his heart stop beating. I'm really grateful for that.

At the VA National Suicide Prevention Center health care providers are on hand around the clock to talk to vets with PTSD and other emotional problems. (**John Berry/ Newhouse News Service/ Landov**)

I let the nuns come in to pray around Dennis, but I wanted to say no. I was enraged that this had happened. This was not right. I did everything I was supposed to do. So why did my husband have to leave the world like that? Why? Why did God allow this to happen? Why does Jean-Marie have to go through this? I kept trying to figure it out, trying to figure out what I could do to undo it. After about three months it started dawning that this was permanent. There was nothing I could do, that this just was, that he was dead.

I couldn't talk to Jean-Marie. I didn't have anything to give her. But she had no outlet. She was talking to people, and I just wanted her to stop. I didn't want anybody to know that he died like that. It was the shame—on top of everything else, it was the shame. When something like this happens, you are so wide open and vulnerable, you have absolutely no defenses. I didn't want my husband's suicide being discussed over coffee at the diner. I didn't want a lot of people knowing, because I couldn't stand to have his death treated casually. And I couldn't defend him because I had nothing. I was just totally, completely an open wound.

> **FAST FACT**
>
> A two-year study by the National Vietnam Veterans Readjustment Survey found that 15.2 percent of male Vietnam veterans and 8.1 percent of female veterans were diagnosed with PTSD.

Understanding Mother and Daughter

It was Jean's idea to go to Sons and Daughters in Touch. The meeting was on Father's Day. You don't know how bad it was on Father's Day because that was the day he shot himself. But we went down there, and we felt welcomed. We were around other people who understood—these people got it. We were standing in line for coffee, and all of a sudden I started crying and I couldn't stop, and I couldn't stop telling people, "My husband shot himself in the head." Jean did the same too, and that's when she really cried. Everyone looked at us with empathy and let us finish. Nobody went, "Oh my God!" They understood. That was such a relief. I was having a hard time getting everything out, and I was falling and choking over what I was saying: "This isn't over, this isn't over. It's 1999, and my husband just died from the Vietnam War."

A Student with PTSD Is Forced to Take a Year Off

Elizabeth Redden

Elizabeth Redden is a Washington, D.C.–based reporter. In the following article she tells the story of Jill Manges, a student at Eastern Illinois University. Redden describes Manges's experience of being suspended from the university after suffering a post-traumatic stress disorder–induced flashback in class. After the flashback episode, Manges was informed by the university that she was being put on a one-year suspension for the safety of herself and others. Although she argued that the suspension was unfair and had her professor testify on her behalf, she was ultimately unsuccessful in being allowed to continue with her classes. Redden also covers the commonality of problems such as this at other universities.

Jill Manges guesses that if she'd suffered an epileptic seizure that day in class, she'd still be enrolled at Eastern Illinois University [EIU]. But Manges, who has post-traumatic stress disorder, instead suffered a flashback during French history that led her to shout and sob uncontrollably.

SOURCE: Elizabeth Redden, "Student, Interrupted," *Inside Higher Ed*, October 15, 2007. Copyright © 2007 Inside Higher Ed. Reproduced by permission.

"I can't deny the fact that what happened was disruptive," says Manges, who was sentenced to a year-long suspension by the university judicial board [in September 2007] for violating two sections of the student conduct code barring the disruption of university functions and the academic environment in particular.

Decisions Are Made

"But I wonder if they would do this to someone who had an epileptic seizure in class or had a hangover in class or had an asthma attack, because that's disruptive too."

In a letter to Manges dated September 17, [2007] Eastern Illinois' assistant director of judicial affairs writes that given Manges' admission that she violated the two code of conduct standards prohibiting disruptive behavior during the September 5 "incident" (in other words, the in-class flashback), and "the seriousness with which the board viewed this incident, it is their recommendation that you be suspended from the university, effective immediately, for a minimum of an academic year through the Spring Semester, 2008, during which you would be prohibited from being on the campus without prior permission of the vice president for student affairs or his designee."

"This was a very difficult decision for the board because they recognize that you have made progress in dealing with the situation but the board is concerned about your well-being as well as the well-being of the greater EIU community. Therefore, the board encourages you to seek a medical withdrawal from the university," the letter continues, indicating that should that be Manges' choice, the board would not submit its suspension recommendation to campus leadership.

"In consequence, as a condition of your readmission to the university," the letter says, "you will need to provide documentation as evidence of your continued improvement and ability to keep your condition under control. . . ."

Eastern Illinois officials won't comment on the specifics of Manges' case. But speaking more broadly about how they handle mental health issues on campus, they stress that they always have students' best interests at heart. "Since we're in such a rural area and some of our services are limited, we realize this may not be the best environment to really serve all students and we also recognize that sometimes a student may not be good in this environment for other students," says Heather Webb, director of judicial affairs at the university.

"Everything is done on a case-by-case basis," says Sandra Cox, the director of the counseling center. "Usually when information goes out there, [people] only have a very small portion of the truth, they have a very small portion of the behaviors that are brought up. They have a very small portion of the whole picture."

A Flashback and Its Fallout

While enrolled at Eastern Illinois, Manges says she saw a private counselor off campus to deal with her diagnosis of PTSD—a result of the sexual abuse she experienced from 1999 through 2000, when someone she knew not only abused her but also collected money from other men who did the same.

She was sitting in French history class September 5 when she could feel a flashback coming. Trying to leave but unable to exit the room in time, she collapsed before reaching the hallway. "I don't remember what happened because I was disassociating, but what witnesses said, what my professor said, is that I started sobbing uncontrollably, shouting, screaming. I was unresponsive; I was just lying on the floor," Manges says.

For the 10 to 15 minutes the episode lasted (of the 50-minute Wednesday afternoon class), the other 15 students "responded by sitting quietly and letting those of us who needed to act do so," says David Smith, the professor teaching the course. "I was extremely proud of how the students responded."

An ambulance came, and Manges declined to go to the hospital. She says it's her understanding that at least two classes, including her French history class, were canceled, and one other was moved. There were six or seven classrooms on the hall, Smith says, and other professors came into the hallway to see what was going on.

Manges experiences such severe flashbacks—which she describes as akin to reliving a traumatizing event—once every two weeks or so. This was the first time one happened in a public academic setting at Eastern Illinois, she says, although she had a similar experience in a classroom at a community college that she previously attended (she transferred to Eastern Illinois in January of [2007]).

Upon returning to her room on September 5, Manges says she had two voice-mail messages waiting: one from judicial affairs, asking her to see a campus counselor, and one from the counseling center. Wanting to comply,

Jill Manges was suspended from Eastern Illinois University for having a PTSD-induced flashback in class. (Zbigniew Bzdak/MCT/Landov)

she called the judicial affairs official, who met Manges to walk her over to the counseling center. The next day, Manges met with judicial affairs for a meeting, and her parents came to the university for a second meeting the day after. "Pretty much the gist of it was she told me how much of a disruption I had caused," Manges says.

Smith, who says that he was interviewed by several college officials about the incident, adds that in his conversations, judicial affairs staff focused on the flashback and the disruption of classes.

A Behavioral Contract Is Signed

After a hearing September 13, Manges says she learned of the year-long suspension and her option to accept a medical withdrawal. She chose the latter so her family could get her tuition money back. Because of that, she says she can't appeal the judicial board's decision. She's living in her off-campus apartment, with plans to get a job, move to Boston in January [2008] and apply to finish college there. She was a junior history major and writing minor at Eastern Illinois. She has no plans to sue, saying she has neither the money nor the time.

Manges says she had come up on judicial affairs' radar screen once previously, back in the spring when she spoke with a professor about experiencing suicidal thoughts. Manges says she was asked by college officials at that time to sign a behavioral contract agreeing to continue psychological treatment and keep up her academic coursework. Manges, who says she is not suicidal now, signed the contract.

She says that she upheld it and that the contract—and the suicidal ideation she experienced in the spring—did not come up during her judicial board hearing, which focused on the PTSD. She says that a letter from her therapist certifies that she is not a threat to herself or others.

And as Gary Pavela, author of *Questions and Answers on College Student Suicide: A Law and Policy Perspective*, points out, "Research indicates that the odds that a student with suicidal ideation will actually commit suicide are 1,000 to one." Several national reports following the 1999 Columbine High School shooting show that "it is inadvisable to create the impression that there is some kind of automatic, hair-trigger response to behavior that is viewed as disruptive or that falls outside of the area of disruptive into suicidal ideation," Pavela says, as the perception of harsh penalties can prevent students from seeking help.

"I don't know what we can do except to make students aware that this is happening at the campus," says Manges, who describes a general lack of awareness of mental health issues. "Honestly, because there's not a lot of knowledge about mental illness, mental illness still has a huge stigma. People don't understand it; people are scared of it because they don't understand it."

"I was certainly disappointed at the outcome," says Smith, the professor of the French history course. He testified on Manges' behalf at the judicial board hearing. "I certainly hoped that the student would be returning to the class, wanted her to come back"—as, he says, did the other students in the course. "I would hope that in the wake of terrible tragedies like at Virginia Tech that universities don't close themselves off as places where students can deal with difficult issues."

Psychology and Behavior

Eastern Illinois administrators say they make a concerted effort to help students deal with their problems while staying on campus. "Whenever possible, we try to work with the student to help them through their mental illness," says Webb, the judicial affairs director. She mentions the behavioral contracts cited by Manges as one example. A number of situations, including excessive alcohol consumption and suicidal ideation, could result in students being asked to sign a contract, which outline a set of expectations.

"It doesn't say we expect you not to experience mental health issues. We expect that," Cox of the counseling center says. "What we look for are changes in behavior."

Webb says that, whenever it's appropriate, she contacts the counseling center to see if a voluntary withdrawal might be an option for a student facing charges in the judicial system. In fact, when asked whether there were any inaccuracies in a student newspaper story outlining Manges' take on what happened, officials clarified a policy stipulating that when mental illness is impacting student behavior, the possibility of a voluntary medical withdrawal is always discussed prior to judicial proceedings.

"[What's been] put out there is that Eastern has suspended students based on mental health reasons. And that is incorrect," says Cox. But, she adds, "if there are long-term or consistent behaviors that are in violation of the student conduct code . . . then we have to look to see, do we have the services for someone who is struggling to a significant extent?"

While Cox says she processes a handful of voluntary withdrawals per week at the university of about 12,000 students, not once in her 11 years at Eastern Illinois has the university had to complete its mandatory withdrawal process for psychological reasons, reserved for the most extreme cases involving threats to the self or others and an inability to take care of oneself.

Yet while Manges technically signed a voluntary withdrawal form, to her it might as well have been mandatory. "I was between a rock and a hard place. I chose a hard place," she says. "I've always been under the impression that people who take a medical withdrawal do it for themselves. For me, it was something that I was pretty much forced into doing."

The Bigger Picture

While what Manges says happened at Eastern Illinois may not be common, nor are such experiences uncommon, says Karen Bower, a senior staff attorney at the Judge David L. Bazelon Center for Mental Health Law. Bower says she routinely (more than once a month) gets calls from students who are forced to leave college for mental health reasons.

"They all feel very betrayed by the school and say that being out of school isn't going to help them," says Bower, who was involved with recent lawsuits on similar issues against George Washington University and Hunter College of the City University of New York that both ended in settlements. "We have urged that schools not use disciplinary action for behavior that's a result of mental illness," Bower says—echoing Professor Smith's sentiment that a judicial board hearing didn't seem like an appropriate venue for addressing his student's situation.

"I am concerned that judicial affairs as a body is designed to handle certain kinds of cases that this kind of event—when someone is not operating in a voluntary manner—they're not well-equipped to deal with," says Smith.

> **FAST FACT**
>
> According to the U.S. Department of Veterans Affairs, women are twice as likely as men to have a diagnosis of PTSD in their lifetime.

In its model policy, the Bazelon Center recommends that involuntary leave only be used in a situation where an individualized assessment determines that a student is a direct threat to the self or others. Under the Americans with Disabilities Act, Bower adds, colleges are required to provide reasonable accommodations for students. That could mean, in this case, she says, waiving the rule about class disruptions for Manges, or mitigating any sentence.

"I think they think it's objective, but discrimination based on conduct that's the result of disability is the same as discrimination based on disability," Bower says. "The use of the disciplinary system as a whole is really a way of removing students from an environment instead of finding out what kinds of supports and services they need to stay in school and be successful."

Although college leaders say they have the students' interests at heart—in addition to the interests of other students—when advocating medical withdrawals, Manges says in her case, at least, the time off won't be helpful. "Being in school is extremely important to me and it is part of the healing process. It is my way of reclaiming my life; it is my way of getting back what was stolen from me when I was younger," says Manges.

"I can't do anything right now. I can work, I can go to therapy, but I was going to therapy while I was in school."

The Iraq War and PTSD

Mary Delach Leonard

Writer Mary Delach Leonard presents the story of Brad Seitz, an Iraq War veteran and former corporal with the First Marine Division. Seitz discusses his battle with PTSD and how open he is with others regarding this illness. He also talks about the attack that led to his PTSD and how he realized that something was wrong in his everyday life. According to Seitz, the Department of Veterans Affairs (VA) has played an important role in his treatment and recovery efforts, especially through group therapy. He states that veterans must be willing to accept help if they are to make any significant progress in dealing with this illness.

Leonard is a staff reporter for *The St. Louis Beacon,* a nonprofit online news publication.

For Iraq War veteran Brad Seitz, the color purple symbolizes five years of life after near-death.

Purple balloons will direct guests to a party this weekend noting the fifth anniversary of the day he earned

SOURCE: Mary Delach Leonard, "Iraq War Vet Celebrates Progress Over PTSD," *St. Louis Beacon*, August, 2008. Copyright © 2008 Saint Louis Beacon. www.stlbeacon.org. Reproduced by permission.

a Purple Heart in service to his country. He will hang out with family and friends at the bowling alley in the recreation center of the Jefferson Barracks VA [Department of Veteran Affairs] Medical Center [St. Louis, Missouri]. Refreshments will include a Purple Heart cake, compliments of the VA.

Seitz, 31, has a fondness for the place. On Thursday nights, the pool, weight room and other facilities are open to all area veterans of the wars in Iraq and Afghanistan. It's a place to find people who understand what he's been through, he said.

Here, too, Seitz has found help to cope with symptoms of post-traumatic stress disorder.

"I just like getting my story out there. I guess I would be considered a good story for the VA. All of my treatment has been excellent," Seitz said. "I think I've gotten the top-notch care that the VA offers. People should know that it's not all bad stories. There are good things that happen."

FAST FACT

A 2003 study in the *New England Journal of Medicine* stated that roughly one in six soldiers returning from Iraq suffered from PTSD.

Wounded in War

Five years ago—on the night of Aug. 13, 2003—Seitz's convoy of Humvees was ambushed by insurgents. Shrapnel from a rocket-propelled grenade peppered his right arm, the explosion knocking him unconscious. He was also shot in the foot during the attack.

Seitz was with the 1st Marine Division that fought its way through Iraq to Baghdad in the early days of the invasion in March 2003. He was among the casualties of the growing insurgency the following summer, wounded just two weeks before he was scheduled to come home.

Much has happened since that night. He got married and is now a mail carrier with the U.S. Postal Service who proudly wears his Marine cap on his rounds. And he welcomes invitations to speak to schools and groups about his experiences in Iraq.

Seitz retired from the Marines with the rank of corporal and 30 percent disability. He credits the VA with helping him learn to cope with PTSD, and he has a message for other veterans who might be reluctant to seek treatment.

Speaking About PTSD

"I have no problem telling someone I have PTSD. It's not a bad word. I went through something that was traumatic. It may take me time to get over it," Seitz said. "The veteran has to want to get the treatment. You have to be proactive in your own recovery from what you went through. You just have to tell somebody you need help, and they'll help you."

These days, Seitz said he is sleeping much better, though he still gets anxious when startled.

The party is a celebration of life, Seitz said. His wife Helen has made an album of his Iraq photos, and they will share their thankfulness that his injuries weren't worse. "I just like hanging out with people," he said. "We'll be bowling and having fun."

Memories of War

Seitz has an outgoing personality and an open approach to life that he believes served him well as a Marine.

"I think I do well in new environments and make new friends easily. I do well with new situations," he said.

Seitz is still a first-wave Marine, speaking on behalf of fellow veterans as he navigates through his own treatment for PTSD. The VA estimates that PTSD occurs in 6 to 11 percent of Afghanistan veterans and 12 to 20 percent of Iraq veterans.

Seitz has a Power Point presentation on Iraq that he is happy to share with interested audiences. He said his pride in his military service has grown stronger over time. "I realize that what I've been through was quite an experience. I was a Marine, and I went to Iraq," he said.

Talking to Young People

He wants youngsters to know that the U.S. military built schools and brought running water and electricity to people in need, and worked to help establish a democratic government.

"When I go to schools I like to tell the kids that it's not just what you see on the news. It's not just about people dying," Seitz said.

He enjoys talking with kids because they aren't afraid to ask questions, even the tough one—whether he killed anyone.

"I tell them I did because I had to," Seitz said. "I made a deal with myself that I wanted to get home, and I would do anything I had to do to make it home. So, yes, I had to. I'm not ashamed of it. I didn't do anything in Iraq I'm not proud of. I kept my nose clean and I did my job and I made it home."

Enlisting After 9/11

Seitz enlisted just months after the terrorist attacks on Sept. 11, 2001. The 1995 graduate of Lafayette High School had been managing a ski and bike shop in Colorado.

"After that happened, I was laying on my couch, and I thought to myself I needed to repay the United States for all the freedoms I've enjoyed my whole life. I just felt I needed to do something," he said.

Seitz told his Marine recruiter that he wanted to join the infantry. "I didn't want to join and sit behind a desk. I wanted to join and fight."

After basic training at Camp Pendleton, Seitz was trained as an infantry mortar man. "We trained like we were going to war," he said. "Every day, we were working with rifles and mortars."

When President George W. Bush gave the order to invade Iraq, the 1st Marine Division was ready. "We did not have a base, no staging points. We were the first ones up," Seitz said. "We just kept moving. We would stop, get out and launch mortars. Then pack everything up and go, moving so fast supply lines couldn't keep up with us."

Because of short supplies, the Marines were limited to one MRE [meal ready to eat] meal a day and as little as an hour and a half of sleep. "We were hungry, tired, thirsty. We had enough water, but it was all chemically cleaned, so you could taste the chlorine in it," Seitz said. "It's war. It's just one of the things they prepared us for. You learn to live on no sleep and little food and little water. It has changed my outlook on things. Being in war and knowing what I went through and that I almost did die, I definitely look at things a lot differently now."

Recounting the Attack

Seitz describes with riveting detail the attack in which he was injured.

He was in the last of a convoy of four unarmored Humvees leaving a jail where they had transported prisoners. A rocket-propelled grenade came through the front window. Seitz, who was riding in back, was knocked unconscious by the explosion.

"I remember opening my eyes, and all I could see was smoke," he said. "You couldn't see in front of your face. It felt like somebody had their hands over my ears. I couldn't hear anything. I had really bad ringing in my ears. While I was unconscious, they had started firing from both sides. You could see the sparks from where the bullets were hitting in the Humvee. I turned, and that's when I got shot in the foot."

He recalls the heavy machine gunfire from the Marines. His friends picking him up to carry him to safety. The Blackhawk helicopter ride to Baghdad for emergency treatment. An emotional phone call home to tell his family what had happened. Medical personnel emailing a photo of his injuries to his girlfriend, now his wife Helen.

Seitz still keeps that photo filed in his Palm Pilot.

It All Happened Quickly

Within weeks of the battle, Seitz was back home in St. Louis on medical leave, awaiting retirement from the Marines. He got married two weeks after returning home and began settling back into civilian life.

Looking back, Seitz knows that he showed symptoms of PTSD, most often triggered by loud noises. But he didn't seek help until after a frightening incident.

"Somebody had lit a firecracker, and it sounded like it was outside my door," he said. "I snapped into Marine Corps mode. I told my wife to get down and to stay low. And that freaked her out. She was scared; she was shaking. My heart rate was pumping. It felt like I was back in the situation. After that, she said, 'You need to go and talk to somebody about this.'"

The next morning, Seitz went to the VA and signed up for treatment. "I'm glad I did it. It was one of the best things I've done since I've gotten back," he said.

Treatment Through the VA

"The St. Louis VA offers various treatment programs for PTSD, tailored to meet individual needs," said counselor Julie Mastnak, a psychologist with the program.

Veterans who contact or are referred to the program are seen within two weeks—or immediately if it is an emergency, she said. The goal is to provide the skills necessary to cope with symptoms. The VA also works with primary-care providers to screen for PTSD.

"There is an increased sensitivity to returning veterans," Mastnak said. "I think there is a real intention that people want to support the veterans coming back."

But, as Seitz points out, the veterans must be willing to accept help. "It takes a lot of courage to acknowledge that something's not the way you want it to be," Mastnak said.

Seitz said he found the group sessions particularly helpful. "When I talk to my wife, she knows—but she

didn't go through it," he said. "She can't really relate to what I saw. It's nice to talk with other people about what you've been through."

Seitz said he embraced the therapy. "I like to think that you get out what you put in. I wasn't going to do it and just sit in the corner and not say anything. Just dive right in and tell everybody what I went through and what happened," he said.

Veterans meet for therapy at the Palo Alto, California, veterans center. The author, an Iraq War veteran, says the VA's programs have helped him to deal with the effects of PTSD.
(AP Images)

Helping Other Veterans

He encourages any veteran who might have issues from combat-related experiences to call the VA.

"I had a friend who was in my unit who lost part of his hand. I called him, and said are you going to the VA? He said no. He doesn't want anything to do with the government. I tell him, 'It would be good for you.' You just have to be around people who understand."

Seitz said veterans shouldn't let concerns about stigmas keep them from getting the treatment they've earned. "I don't see how it would hurt you to tell someone you have an illness or PTSD," he said. "There might be some guys out there who think you're going to be looked down on because you're weak or you're not tough enough to handle what you went through. If I see a problem, I fix it. If you need help, get it."

The nightmares have lessened, Seitz said. "I was sleeping maybe an hour-and-a-half a night. It was taking its toll, and I was constantly tired. I couldn't fall asleep. Then I would get flashbacks of when I got injured and that scenario. And then [there] were crazy dreams of people from out of nowhere launching rockets at me. I was running and seeing rockets flying," he said. "I have been sleeping a lot more now."

Seitz said the treatment isn't just about him. "I'm not doing it just for me, I'm doing it for my whole family," he said.

Late-Onset Post-Traumatic Stress Disorder

Howard Reich

In the following selection author Howard Reich describes his experience of trying to find information on late-onset post-traumatic stress disorder. Reich's mother, Sonia, began experiencing PTSD symptoms almost sixty years after her experiences in the Holocaust during World War II. Reich discusses the background regarding late-onset PTSD and talks about Holocaust survivors and how they differ from other PTSD sufferers. He also details the dramatic differences between the experiences of children and adult survivors and how children do not have the family connections or coping mechanisms that so often can help adults. He concludes by describing the reaction of society to these children and how that reaction adds an extra burden to the already suffering children.

Howard Reich is a writer for *The Chicago Tribune*.

To my dismay, there wasn't a single book written on late-onset PTSD, nor one story in all the newspaper databases I scoured. But by interviewing PTSD

SOURCE: Howard Reich, *The First and Final Nightmare of Sonia Reich: A Son's Memoir*, Cambridge, MA: Public Affairs, 2006. Copyright © 2006 by Howard Reich. Reprinted by permission of Public Affairs, a member of Perseus Books, L.L.C.

specialists around the world, I was able to find what I was searching for—scientific corroboration of what I had observed in my mother's behavior and what [her physician] Dr. Rosenberg had confirmed in his evaluation. A few dozen articles penned by psychiatric researchers conveyed hard data—scant but precious—about people like my mother whose traumatic childhoods had come raging back at them.

"Survivor Syndrome" Is Part of PTSD

As early as 1964, a psychiatrist named William Niederland had identified an entire subset of PTSD victims—those who escaped death in the Holocaust but showed symptoms of what he coined "survivor syndrome." The survivor syndrome characteristics looked like a blueprint of my mother's problems and could include "increased arousal," "confusion between the present and the period of persecution (acting or feeling as if the traumatic event were recurring)," "psychotic and psychotic-like symptoms (illusions and hallucinations)," and "inability to verbalize the nature of the events," wrote Dr. Joel Sadavoy in a journal of psychiatry.

> **FAST FACT**
>
> According to the Anti-Defamation League 1.5 million children were murdered during the Holocaust.

Moreover, "individuals with PTSD may also find themselves, or place themselves, in stressful situations, possibly to fulfill a compulsion to repeat trauma," noted Dr. Rachel Yehuda and colleagues in another journal article on the same subject.

Though the lack of widespread awareness of late-onset PTSD meant there had been a dearth of systematic studies, the few that existed contained devastating data.

In one analysis of two hundred Holocaust survivors, 85 percent showed survivor syndrome twenty to thirty years after the war, reported Sadavoy. In a 1969 study of 130 patients "who were believed to show no after-effects of the concentration camp experience," Sadavoy noted, the researcher P. Matussek "observed that, on closer inquiry, he did not see a single person in this group who was without pathology."

Difficult Stories to Hear

Most survivors had not sought psychiatric help after the war, nor were they encouraged to. The world could not bear to hear their stories, society at large making it clear to survivors that they simply should get on with their lives.

Even psychiatrists, the studies said, found the survivors' stories difficult to hear and often dissuaded patients from exploring them, helping to weave a "curtain of silence" around the subject, in the phrasing of Milton E. Jucovy in a journal of psychoanalysis. "It seemed necessary for both survivors and the external world to forget," wrote Jucovy. "Denial and repression reigned during this period of silence."

Even had the survivors sought psychiatric help, it may not have altered their fates. Because it was hard for them to trust, it was also difficult for them to put much faith in anyone else understanding their pain, many psychiatrists observed. When the survivors did attempt to explain their half-buried experiences, they often could not bear to.

Ultimately, they were caught in a trap, since the elderly inevitably look back to take stock of their pasts and assess how they have lived their lives. "The trouble is that in the process of reviewing one's life, as the memories are restored . . . and are owned up to (in other words, in the process of the return of the repressed) the individual experiences pain," wrote Dr. Henry Krystal, a pioneer in the field and a Holocaust survivor himself. Those memories, added Krystal, "are so intense, threatening and painful that one must ward them off by deadening oneself or abort the process by escaping into denial. . . .

"I have to admit that my attempts to engage aging survivors of the Holocaust in psychoanalytic psychotherapy have been for the most part unsuccessful."

Suppressing the Past

Research on the subject indicated that there were many people who appeared to have led normal lives—getting married, raising children, welcoming grandchildren—before facing the delayed consequences of their devastated childhoods.

As psychiatric researchers began investigating these phenomena in the 1980s and '90s, they kept extending the length of time in which they believed a survivor could suppress the past before being overcome by it. Dr. Haim Dasberg, a PTSD expert based in Jerusalem, summed up the dawning awareness of the problem in a revelatory, unpublished paper that he emailed to me. In 1994, researcher H. Bower noticed depression and anxiety among survivors after more than three decades of latency, wrote Dasberg. Three years later, Prof. B. Schreuder observed that "it is repeatedly demonstrated to us that even after 40 years, intrusive re-experiencing is still present or has returned after years without symptoms." And in 1997, "H. Spiro et al. mentions 'numerous' case reports on delayed PTSD among POWs [prisoners of war] and ex-soldiers, even after 50 years," noted Dasberg.

Over Sixty Years Later

My mother, however, may have beat them all, waiting fifty-six years after the war—and fully sixty-two years since the Russians invaded her "little Dubno"—until her past took hold of her present.

The PTSD analysts did more, however, than observe a new psychiatric phenomenon: they drew conclusions as to why late-onset PTSD was occurring. Essentially, Holocaust survivors were forced to fend for themselves after the war, and they rose to the challenge, putting aside—as much as was possible—the horrors of the past. They invented "what may be termed a traumatically induced 'false self,'" wrote Sadavoy, referring to "a form of character armor, protecting the victim's vulnerable true self that was impinged upon by the trauma.

"The false self meets the world successfully when supported by life circumstances such as stable marriage, having and raising children, immersion in activities and friendships, work and good health. But the traumatically affected part of the self lies vulnerable beneath the surface; emotions and thoughts are waiting to be tripped."

Other psychiatrists referred to the "splitting" between "a traumatized inner core and outward adaptation," as Dasberg put it.

Though survivors who were young and strong and preoccupied with busy lives could put their memories aside, the cumulative stress of suppressing their pasts for decades, as well as the encroaching infirmities of old age, made it increasingly difficult to continue the fight. "Ever

Two Korean War veterans attend a PTSD group therapy session. PTSD symptoms sometimes do not appear until decades after the traumatic event occurred. (Zia Nizami/ MCT/Landov)

greater amounts of energy are required to meeting ego functions," wrote Dori Laub and Nanette C. Auerhahn, "until real life becomes a fringe phenomenon around the nucleus of the trauma."

Mourning and Memories

Most of the few dozen papers on the subject concurred that the devastation suffered by child survivors—77 percent of whom lost both parents—was so great that mourning was virtually impossible. For mourning was designed for loss, the natural—although difficult—cycles of life and death, not catastrophes of incomprehensible magnitude. Like parents who never can reconcile themselves to the death of a child, survivors could not easily accept or "integrate" their losses and simply move on. Their grief was "unresolved and unresolvable," in the words of Sadavoy, their only tools for dealing with it being denial, repression, and splitting.

Yet the memories, though buried deep, never really went away. They lingered, causing insomnia, nightmares, and a host of psychosomatic illnesses, from upset stomach to chronic headache. Though often "subclinical," as doctors referred to levels of anxiety that may not have been readily apparent or easily diagnosed, these symptoms gave expression to the terrifying memories that played upon the survivors' emotional stability.

Differences in PTSD

Among trauma sufferers, Holocaust survivors may have been particularly vulnerable to the delayed-onset effect, for their profile was so different from soldiers in war. While Vietnam veterans with PTSD developed a "warrior syndrome" that often expressed itself in "belligerence, violence, suspiciousness, poor work history, severely disrupted interpersonal relationship, drugs and alcohol abuse, risk-taking behaviors, psychopathological disorders and self-destructive, marginal lifestyles," wrote

Sadavoy, the Holocaust survivors appeared to blend in with their new worlds.

The difference, researchers believed, may have been due to the fact that veterans had faced trauma on the battlefield as uniformed combatants armed to kill, often extending their violent patterns of behavior afterward. Holocaust survivors, by contrast, were unarmed civilians who had no comparable outlet for expressing their fears and had to "resort to passive suppression of rage or other emotions," wrote Sadavoy, paraphrasing B. Goderez. After the war, the survivors continued drawing upon their already formidable strengths at tamping down their anger and shame, some earning the macabre psychiatric term "super repressors" for their ability to deny conscious awareness of their own pasts. . . .

The Suffering of Children

Among those who suffered and survived the Holocaust, none may have endured more anguish as it played out, or afterward, than children. Though only a few scientific papers touched on the particular psychological perils of PTSD among child survivors, those that did offered haunting perspectives.

"As [Sarah] Moskovitz (1983) discusses so poignantly, 'The loss of parents in early life means loss of the very nucleus of one's own identity,'" wrote Dr. Robert Krell, himself a child survivor, in a journal of child psychiatry. Moskovitz, continued Krell, mentions "'the continuing burden of loss the survivors feel for parents whom they have never known, a hunger for some link with the past through family connections destroyed or distorted, for traces of themselves buried in childhoods they dare not remember.'"

As I read these words, I instantly recalled my father lamenting that he hadn't saved photos of his parents and wished he could see once again what they looked like. My mother was nearly a decade younger than he and perhaps had even fainter recollections of her earliest years, before the war, and of the people who once nurtured her.

"The child survivors may have no memory [of their pre-Holocaust past]," wrote Krell. "Too young to have partaken of a foundation for life, too traumatized to experience a childhood, too preoccupied with survival to reflect on its impact, the child survivors were not blessed with the opportunity for the systematized, chronological collection of ordinary personal history."

Instead, Krell said, the children spent their formative years leading anarchic lives. They often witnessed atrocities that adults did not, because children were small and could see without being seen.

Society Turns Its Back

During the war, society had turned against these children, and they were left at the mercy of Christians who might save them for awhile or turn them in to authorities to be killed. Even when successfully hidden, the children's lives were turbulent, since most spent the Holocaust hiding with several different families. Because the majority of child survivors were twice orphaned, they eventually landed in adoptive families or foster homes, where they took pains to hide their pasts. For although "the elder survivor is more likely to retain a sense of pride in survivorhood," noted Krell in a journal of child psychiatry, the children felt something opposite.

"The younger survivor finds little pride and no dignity in survivorhood," wrote Krell. "As children, they experienced degradation and humiliation from their Christian neighbors, particularly other children."

A Double Tragedy

So they kept quiet about their pain and shame. But even if they had railed on about it, they would have found few willing to listen. The world at large—and the scientific community in particular—was eager to assist in their denial, with some German psychiatrists, in particular, maintaining that persecuted children could not remember their pasts and therefore could not have been permanently harmed by it, wrote Milton Kestenberg and others. Kestenberg was quick to point out that even if child survivors did forget portions of their pasts, that loss inevitably represented a form of psychological damage.

But it wasn't only some German doctors who minimized their scars. "They have been told by older survivors that the children were lucky to have avoided slave labor and then live after the war in an orphanage where they were well fed and didn't have to fend for themselves," observed Sarah Moskovitz in a psychiatric journal.

In yet one more impediment to a peaceful postwar existence, the child victims did not realize the profundity of their problems. As Dasberg wrote, "child survivors have no insight or awareness of the fact that they are damaged or disordered," since they had scant frame of reference for what an ordinary childhood and adolescence looked like.

The toll of this double tragedy—psychological damage inflicted upon victims who remained unaware of it—was a constantly deepening burden of pain.

The Unique Issues of a Female War Veteran

Angela Peacock

In the following selection army veteran Angela Peacock describes her experiences in South Korea and Iraq that led to post-traumatic stress disorder. As an eighteen-year-old recruit, she was stationed in South Korea where she was raped by a noncommissioned officer. Later, after being posted to Iraq, she began to lose weight and was sent for a medical evaluation. Following this evaluation, which included a mental health assessment, Peacock was medically retired from the armed forces. Peacock discusses the progress she has made in her recovery and how far she still has to go.

I was an 18-year old, fresh out of high school, with an M16 [rifle] and camouflage paint smeared on my face, excited, a little naïve at just what I had gotten myself into.

No one told me that eleven years later, I'd be tired, very broken, isolated, and damaged goods. Yes, I was assaulted and harassed while serving my country. No one

SOURCE: Angela Peacock, "To Hell and Back Again," The Huffington Post, November 24, 2008. Reproduced by permission.

warned me that joining the Army made me twice as likely to be sexually assaulted than my civilian counterparts. That's not what I was signing up for.

Angela's Background

I come from a family where military service makes you a man (or a woman, in my case). Both grandparents served in the Army Air Corps in World War II and my father dreamed of being in the Navy. Plans changed for him when I was born and he broke his leg in a motorcycle accident. I wanted to travel to crazy places few people have ever heard of or even knew existed. I wanted to meet those people I would see in *National Geographic* commercials or the *World Almanac* my grandfather would show me when I was little. Most of all, I wanted to get out of St. Louis and experience life on this irresistible planet.

I wanted to declare my independence to everyone I knew, so I shaved my head and signed the dotted line. A little rebellious I guess, but I liked the excitement of it all!

I had been a born leader, tough as a brick shithouse, and could knock boys over when I played soccer with them in the neighborhood. I played all the sports, ran faster than most guys and could outwit anyone with their intellectual theories. Especially the Catholic Republican in my Advanced English class senior year who would debate with me on issues such as abortion, the death penalty, and who would be President of the United States first, him or I.

In 1997, my senior year, *GI Jane* came out. I watched it the night before I left for the Army and dreamed of being just like Demi Moore, just as tough as the guys, I was ready, willing, and able to do anything a "man" could do.

Years Later

Eleven years later, I wound up 2100 miles from home, staying in a homeless veterans shelter, attending a three month Renew Program for women veterans who have experienced Military Sexual Trauma with Post-traumatic

Stress Disorder. There were only five women in my group who were willing to face all the pain of their past to come out feeling better on the other side. Who says women aren't strong?

There, I met Amanda Spain, producer of *In Their Boots*, an online documentary series showing the struggles of Iraq and Afghanistan vets when we come home. They are apolitical, and funded by a grant from the Iraq Afghanistan Deployment Impact fund (IADIF) and produced by Brave New Foundation under Robert Greenwald.

She asked me if I'd be willing to share my story with those that were willing to listen. Apprehensive, and shocked that someone finally cared enough to listen, I hesitatingly agreed.

It was the first time, ever, to share my story, from beginning to end.

Raped by a Trusted NCO

One night in South Korea, I went out with some friends to the "Ville" which is all the little hole-in-the-wall bars and restaurants right outside the gates of Camp Carroll, Waegwan, South Korea. It was a dark, spring night and I had to work the next morning at 0730 hours to complete my yearly Common Tasks Training with the unit. I went out for an hour or so, only had one small drink, as being drunk was not my cup of tea at the time. I went to leave an hour later and someone had stolen my keys. Nervous, I walked through the gate with a male, non-commissioned officer [NCO] I had seen around but didn't know very well. We are taught to respect and trust the NCO's and I had no reason not to. You are not allowed in South Korea to walk through the streets alone as it is with Armed Forces Policy in most places overseas. My roommate was not in our room so I decided to stay in the NCO's room down the hall to wait for her to come home. I checked several times throughout the night but no answer from my roommate.

The male asks me four times to have sex with him and I say no all four times. First, I tell him I don't know him, then I tell him I have a boyfriend in Germany, then I tell him again I don't know him. The final time, I tell him I am on my period and NO! Next thing I remember is my naked body being violently thrown all over the bed and I am unable to scream or stop it. I don't know, to this day, if I was drugged or hit over the head.

I remember hearing his roommate, just on the other side of the room and I am trying to scream, but nothing comes out. It is as if I am out of my body watching from across the room and can do absolutely nothing to get back in my body and fight him off.

I wake up the next morning twenty minutes late for my 0730 formation. Shaken, not quite sure what happened that night I am standing naked in the bathroom and cannot unwedge the tampon that is shoved all the way up.

My Platoon Leader asks me what's wrong and did I drink too much the night before, he smells my breath and concedes that that's not it, but what is it? I don't even know.

The Remembering Begins

Three days later, I get flashes and cold chills as I am standing in the office and see him. My body knew what happened before I did. Somehow, I am told, the body remembers. My hands are shaking and sweaty and now it's all clear. It's too late for a rape kit, I had to tell someone.

I talk to my Platoon Sergeant, the man I respected the most. He told me that in the military when there is a rape trial they will blame it on me and make it look like I was asking for it. They would say I drank too much, I was a party girl. They would make up lies and I would be on trial, not the NCO. As I am a naïve 21-year old who trusts her leaders, I go along with his plan to just "live with it." My Platoon Sergeant told me the only thing that would happen to him would be that his rank would be

The viewpoint's author, Angela Peacock, relates her experiences about being sexually assaulted while serving in the U.S. armed forces and how the event changed her life. (AP Images)

knocked down one level, he would be transferred back to the States and I would have to live the rest of my life with it. So I stuff it way down inside and begin my new way of coping with it, binge drinking on the weekends.

Six months later, I reenlisted to stay in four more years and signed up for Europe. September 11th happens and I know Europe will be the first to deploy when war breaks out. We all knew it was coming. I will leave a part of myself in Korea.

A year and a half later, May 6, 2003, I am driving in a convoy from Kuwait to Baghdad. My family is watching it all back home on CNN and they have no idea.

I already had pain in me from the assault and now I am being exposed to the horrors of war. No front lines for women, my ass. Baghdad is the front line. No, I didn't have to kill anyone, but the fear of thinking today could be my last, either from running over an IED [improvised explosive device], small arms fire from a sniper, a grenade being thrown from the overpasses or the fact that my Tactical Signal Unit has no armored plates in our flak jackets like the contractors get.

I hear stories of soldiers killing themselves in port-a-potties, crazy Iraqis blowing themselves up and what happened the day before in the "Underpass of Death" outside a market we frequent on our way to the Green Zone for supply pickup three times a week.

Falling Apart and Holding It In

I am having panic attacks daily, nightmares, flashbacks, all things I don't find out the names for until I get back to Germany. I kept a journal of me losing my mind. Fevers, diarrhea, vomiting, bloody noses, losing 48 pounds in two months.

Supply lines are not steady yet and we get 1 liter of water a day and the temperature is 130 degrees in the shade. I am falling apart.

My Command will not send me back to get medical treatment as I am "mission essential." Finally, I get orders to Fort Lewis, Washington, as there is some loophole somewhere that says you can not be overseas more than 3 years straight. I get medevac'd [flown out] two weeks early for medical treatment.

When I arrive back at Landstuhl Hospital in Germany, they run every test possible to see why I lost all that weight, as I am now a withering 103 pounds. No one asks me if it could be emotional or combat induced.

After seeing a fellow soldier from my unit, who now had staples from his chest to his genitals, I lose it and walk myself to psychiatry. I still tried to hold it all in, only telling the Major that every time I hear a door slam I think it is a gunshot. Be strong, I tell myself, I am tough. I can handle this.

I get to Fort Lewis a month later to find out my new unit is being deployed in two months, I am going back to Baghdad.

Two weeks into redeployment, I get double ear infections, a fever, and chills. I am ordered by the Medical Staff to report to Mental Health section as when they see my pulse rate is 140 beats per minute and my blood pressure is through the roof, I am having a panic attack, and can't hide it anymore. Their stupid machines caught me covering it up.

Out of the Army

I walk to Mental Health and explode. Holding nothing back the Triage Doctor tells me I am not allowed to be around weapons as I am now a danger to myself. I am non-deployable and will be medically boarded out of the Army.

I am angry, confused, the Army is my life. I am a Sergeant, my soldiers need me and I need them. I just wanted help, I didn't want to be discharged. I had served 7 years and wanted to retire from the Army.

The day I was medically retired, I laid on the couch all day knowing my life was over. I was 25 years old. I went from war hero to piece of shit in one day. I was depressed, couldn't sleep, and my husband, also an Iraq vet, didn't know how to help me or what was even wrong. Little did we know, we both had PTSD, for different reasons, but nonetheless, we waged our own war against each other in the same house.

The next two years are fogged from my use of prescription drugs to numb myself. I didn't want to feel anything. I wish I had died in Iraq. At least the deceased aren't suffering. I am trapped in my mind reliving over and over the rape and the war. I am not sure if I am even alive.

My husband finally gives up on me a year later and tells me to move back home, that I need my family to help me because he can't get through to me. I am addicted to numbing my pain with anything that will stop it, even for a minute a day.

The year of 2006, I attempt suicide more times than I can count. I argue with God to just take me. I trap myself in my house and push my family away. I am ready to die.

After four months of feeling myself die on the inside, I finally check in for the fourth and final time to get clean and sober and tell them everything. If this doesn't work, I decide, I am jumping off the tallest building in St. Louis.

PTSD Recovery

I have now been in recovery for drug addiction and Post-Traumatic Stress Disorder for two years. I have not attempted suicide once in that period of time. I am more proud of that than my military service. I have given up on organized religion to help me answer the questions my mind has posed, like, "Why me?" The pure part in the deepest part of my soul, which knows none of this was ever my fault, and didn't deserve any of it, has kept me alive. I can say that there must be a God that has saved me from a hell which I created in my own mind, and given me a second chance at living one day at a time. It has been a very slow crawl back, and I am just getting started. I still cannot trust, I still cannot sleep, I still have awful memories, nightmares and imaginings of things so horrible I cannot say them here.

> **FAST FACT**
>
> Of the women who have served in Iraq, 8 to 10 percent suffer from post-traumatic stress disorder.

But I do have hope and a dog that has helped me cope. I have courage that things will get a little easier every day and that someday, the wounds of rape and war will be healed inside me.

There are thousands just like me, women and men, veterans who signed up to serve their country and were raped, tortured, harassed, and raped again by their command.

When I enlisted in the Army I took an oath to support and defend the Constitution of the United States against all enemies, foreign and domestic. My oath did not end upon discharge. I want to help other men and women veterans get the support that they need and know there is hope that we can get better. We must not give up. We must band together and make sure this doesn't happen to our sons and daughters.

GLOSSARY

anxiety | Feelings of fear or apprehension that have the physical symptoms of irregular heart rhythms, sweating, and overwhelming stress.

battle fatigue | The name given to PTSD symptoms suffered by soldiers who served in World War II and Korea.

cognitive behavioral therapy | PTSD therapy that helps the individual change his or her thoughts regarding the trauma experience.

combat fatigue | The name given to PTSD symptoms suffered by soldiers who served in World War I.

comorbidity | Physical symptoms or disease that accompany, but are unrelated to, another existing ailment.

debriefing | A conversation with the victim of a traumatic event to help that person deal with what occurred. This conversation is most effective when conducted by a professional trained in debriefing techniques.

depression | Sadness or melancholy that exceeds normal amounts of these emotions, including negative thoughts, moods, and behaviors. The intensity of these symptoms can impact day-to-day life and cause functional disabilities.

dissociation | The distancing of the mind from the body or emotions resulting in certain conditions such as amnesia or hysteria.

EMDR | See eye movement desensitization and reprocessing.

epidemic | A disease or illness that affects a disproportionately large number of individuals at the same time.

exposure therapy | Repeatedly talking with a therapist about a traumatic event so an individual can come to terms with the feelings and thoughts about the trauma.

eye movement desensitization and reprocessing	PTSD therapy that involves focusing the eyes on the therapist's hand movements while discussing traumatic memories.
group therapy	A group session with a trained therapist that usually includes six to ten individuals dealing with the same kinds of issues or situations. The group uses each member's experiences to help deal with their own difficulties.
hormone	A chemical produced in the body that regulates the activity of other cells and/or organs.
ideographic	A symbol used to represent words or a concept.
intervention	Confronting an individual about his or her destructive behavior and how it is affecting others.
irritable heart	The name given to PTSD symptoms suffered by soldiers who served in the Civil War.
malingering	Intentionally faking or exaggerating physical ailments for personal gain.
neurotransmitters	Chemicals that relay signals between neurons by traveling across the nerve synapses. These chemicals trigger certain responses in the receptor cells.
nostalgia	The name given to PTSD symptoms suffered by soldiers who served in the Civil War.
panic attack	Sudden periods of acute anxiety or intense fear developing for no apparent reason. These episodes usually happen only rarely in an individual's lifetime.
panic disorder	A type of chronic anxiety disorder characterized by frequent panic attacks.
psychiatry	The branch of medicine that studies and treats mental disorders.
psychological trauma	Severe distress or shock from experiencing a disastrous or traumatic event.

psychotherapy	The treatment of psychological disorders. Can include such treatments as group therapy, psychoanalysis, or behavioral therapy.
shell shock	A term used in World War I to describe the psychological trauma occurring among soldiers facing active and prolonged combat.
somatization	Converting mental experiences into physical symptoms.
stress	The reaction of an individual to the outside factors affecting his or her life. How a person responds to stress can increase or decrease the effect of these forces.

CHRONOLOGY

B.C.   **1500**   Egyptian soldier Hori describes his feelings before going into battle and how they affected him.

  800   In Homer's *Iliad* the character Achilles experiences all-consuming rage in response to battle experiences.

  480   Greek historian Herodotus describes how Spartan commander Leonidas dismissed some of his soldiers before the battle of Thermopylae Pass because they were psychologically exhausted from previous battles.

A.D.   **1666**   Englishman Samuel Pepys describes the horror, fear, and psychological aftereffects of the Great Fire of London.

  1700s   Studies are done on symptoms exhibited by railroad accident survivors.

  early 1800s   Doctors begin diagnosing soldiers with "exhaustion" when they exhibit the symptoms of what will become post-traumatic stress disorder.

  1865   During the Civil War, soldiers are diagnosed with "irritable heart" or "nostalgia" when they exhibit PTSD-like symptoms.

  1870s   Neurologist Jean-Martin Charcot begins a study of the mental disorder hysteria.

1891 One-third of the federal budget is spent on military pensions. Sufferers of "nostalgia" or "irritable heart" have great difficulty qualifying for benefits.

1890s Frenchman Pierre Janet theorizes that traumatic symptoms are directly related to a damaging experience that had overwhelmed the mind.

1915 During this year of World War I, more than twenty thousand British soldiers are admitted to hospitals with behavioral disorders that do not seem to have a cause.

1916 Medical officer Charles Myers coins the term "shell shock" to describe the psychiatrically troubled soldiers he has been treating.

1952 Stress response syndrome is listed in the first edition of the *Diagnostic and Statistical Manual of Mental Disorders*.

1968 Psychoanalyst Henry Krystal studies the effects of trauma on concentration camp survivors and publishes his findings in *Massive Psychic Trauma*.

1969 Six presentations by professor of psychiatry Harry S. Abram at a University of Virginia psychological stress symposium are edited into *Psychological Aspects of Stress*. Abram is considered by many to be one of the main contributors in defining PTSD and its symptoms.

1976 Psychiatrist Mardi J. Horowitz publishes *Stress Response Syndromes: PTSD, Grief and Adjustment Disorders*. This work is one of the first to describe the processes of stress response and the treatment of stress symptoms.

1980 The American Psychiatric Association adds PTSD to the third edition of its *Diagnostic and Statistical Manual of Mental Disorders.*

1983 The National Vietnam Veterans Readjustment Study is conducted to study the prevalence of PTSD and other psychological issues among Vietnam veterans.

1989 The National Center for PTSD is created in the Department of Veterans Affairs.

1994 In the diagnostic criteria for PTSD listed in the fourth edition of the *Diagnostic and Statistical Manual of Mental Disorders,* the definition of a traumatic event—formerly described as a nomothetic, or generalized, event—is redefined as an idiopathic event, or one unique to an individual.

2000 Congress establishes the National Child Traumatic Stress Network (NCTSN).

2007 The number of American service members diagnosed with PTSD increases 50 percent over 2006 levels.

2009 The National Institutes of Health recruit participants for fifteen new studies involving PTSD.

ORGANIZATIONS TO CONTACT

The editors have compiled the following list of organizations concerned with the issues debated in this book. The descriptions are derived from materials provided by the organizations. All have publications or information available for interested readers. The list was compiled on the date of publication of the present volume; the information provided here may change. Be aware that many organizations take several weeks or longer to respond to inquiries, so allow as much time as possible.

Anxiety Disorder Association of America (ADAA)
6000 Executive Blvd.
Rockville, MD 20852
(301) 231-9350
www.adaa.org

A nonprofit organization, ADAA focuses on the prevention, treatment, and cure of anxiety disorders and improving the daily life of individuals suffering from these conditions. It publishes self-help books and informational brochures on all aspects of anxiety disorders. Its Web site offers detailed information on the various types of disorders and also offers downloadable reports and papers.

Gift from Within
16 Cobb Hill Rd.
Camden, ME 04843
(207) 236-8858
fax: (207) 236-2818
www.giftfromwithin
.org

This nonprofit support organization focuses on PTSD sufferers, their families, and those at risk for PTSD. They offer peer support services, personal coping aids, and lists of trauma survivor support groups. DVDs, books, articles, pamphlets, and other educational materials are available through its Web site.

International Society for Traumatic Stress Studies
111 Deer Lake Rd.
Ste. 100, Deerfield, IL 60015
(847) 480-9028
fax: (847) 480-9282
www.istss.org

The International Society for Traumatic Stress Studies focuses on the exchange of information about severe trauma and stress, including research, public policy, and education. The society publishes the *Journal of Traumatic Stress* several times per year. Its Web site offers resources for the general public, including information about traumatic stress, links to other organizations, video downloads, and informational pamphlets.

National Center for PTSD (NCPTSD)
Department of Veterans Affairs
215 N. Main St.
White River Junction VT 05009-0001
(802) 295-9363
866/OUR VETS
PTSD Information Line: (802) 296-6300
ncptsd@va.gov

NCPTSD, part of the Office of Mental Health Services, focuses on the clinical care and welfare of American veterans suffering from PTSD and research and educational programs related to traumatic stress. The organization offers in-depth information on all aspects of PTSD, including diagnosis and assessment, treatment, family issues, and other psychological and medical problems related to traumatic stress. Various publications are available upon request.

National Child Traumatic Stress Network (NCCTS)
University of California, Los Angeles
11150 W. Olympic Blvd., Ste. 650, Los Angeles, CA 90064
(310) 235-2633
fax: (310) 235-2612

NCCTS, operated by the University of California at Los Angeles (UCLA) and Duke University under the umbrella of the U.S. Department of Health and Human Services, focuses on increasing access to medical and mental health services for families with children suffering from trauma. The organization concentrates on raising the standards of medical care in relation to children and PTSD. Its Web site offers detailed information on various types of trauma and other aspects of PTSD. Pamphlets and fact sheets are available.

National Institute of Mental Health (NIMH)
Science Writing, Press, and Dissemination Branch
6001 Executive Blvd.
Rm. 8184, MSC 9663
Bethesda, MD
20892-9663
(301) 443-4513
(866) 615-6464
fax: (301) 443-4279
www.nimh.nih.gov

NIMH, part of the National Institutes of Health, emphasizes research focused on overall mental health and the understanding, treatment, and prevention of mental disorders. The institute provides detailed information on all types of mental disorders, and free information is available upon request. Clinical studies information is available through its Web site along with statistics and medication information. Its companion Web site, Medline Plus, offers a large amount of detailed information on many different aspects of PTSD.

FOR FURTHER READING

Books

Victoria Lemle Beckner and John B. Arden, *Conquering Post-Traumatic Stress Disorder*. Beverly, MA: Fair Winds, 2008.

Chris R. Brewin, *Posttraumatic Stress Disorder: Malady or Myth?* New Haven, CT: Yale University Press, 2007.

Matthew Friedman, *Post-Traumatic and Acute Stress Disorders*. Kansas City, MO: Compact Clinicals, 2003.

James Whitney Hicks, *50 Signs of Mental Illness*. New Haven, CT: Yale University Press, 2005.

David Kinchin, *Post Traumatic Stress Disorder: The Invisible Injury*. Oxfordshire, UK: Success Unlimited, 2004.

Diane Peters Mayer, *The Everything Guide to Controlling Anxiety*. Avon, MA: Adams Media, 2005.

Richard Mollica, *Healing Invisible Wounds: Paths to Hope and Recovery in a Violent World*. Orlando, FL: Harcourt, 2006.

Frank Parkinson, *Post-Trauma Stress*. Cambridge, MA: DaCapo, 2000.

Glenn R. Schiraldi, *The Post-Traumatic Stress Disorder Sourcebook*. New York: McGraw-Hill, 2000.

Edward Tick, *War and the Soul: Healing Our Nation's Veterans from Post-traumatic Stress Disorder*. Wheaton, IL: Quest, 2005.

Elise Forbes Tripp, *Surviving Iraq: Soldiers' Stories*. Northampton, MA: Olive Branch, 2008.

Mary Beth Williams and Soili Poijula, *The PTSD Workbook*. Oakland, CA: New Harbinger, 2002.

Trish Wood, *What Was Asked of Us: An Oral History of the Iraq War by the Soldiers Who Fought It*. New York: Little Brown, 2006.

Periodicals

Benedict Carey, "Review of Landmark Study Finds Fewer Vietnam Veterans with Post-Traumatic Stress, *New York Times*, August 18, 2006.

Tori DeAngelis, "PTSD Treatments Grow in Evidence, Effectiveness," *Monitor on Psychology*, vol. 39, no. 1, January 2008.

Nancy Gibbs, "Our Armies, Ourselves," *Time*, vol. 171, no. 21, May 26, 2008.

Alex Kingsbury, "Living with an Asterisk," *U.S. News & World Report*, vol. 143, no. 7, September 3, 2007.

Deborah Kotz, "Relax! Stress, If Managed, Can Be Good for You," *U.S. News & World Report*, vol. 144, no. 17, June 16, 2008.

Susan Kruglinski, "How to Erase a Single Memory," *Discover*, January 2008.

Alex Markels, "Recovery's Long Road," *U.S. News & World Report*, vol. 142, no. 15, April 30, 2007.

Susan Mayor, "Psychological Therapy Is Better than Debriefing for PTSD," *British Medical Journal*, vol. 330, no. 7493, March 26, 2005.

Anna Mulrine, "Years of Hardship Take a Toll on Families," *U.S. News & World Report*, vol. 145, no. 1, July 7–July 14, 2008.

Carol Smith, "Broken Warrior: One Soldier's Struggle," *Seattle Post-Intelligencer*, April 13, 2007.

Mark Thompson, "America's Medicated Army," *Time*, vol. 171, no. 24, June 16, 2008.

United States Congress, "Working in a War Zone: Post Traumatic Stress Disorder in Civilians Returning from Iraq: Hearing Before the Subcommittee on the Middle East and South Asia of the Committee on Foreign Affairs, House of Representatives, One Hundred Tenth Congress, first session, June 19, 2007."

William M. Welch, "Trauma of Iraq War Haunting Thousands Returning Home," *USA Today*, February 28, 2005.

Internet Sources

Associated Press, "Sept. 11 Attacks Left 70,000 with Stress Disorder," MSNBC, September 10, 2008. www.msnbc.msn.com/id/26645918.

————, "Smoking Worsens PTSD Symptoms, Say Doctors," MSNBC, January 26, 2009. www.msnbc.msn.com/id/28859829.

J. Douglas Bremner, "Stressing the Hippocampus: Why It Matters," *Scientific American*, January 8, 2008. www.sciam.com/blog/60-second-science.cfm.

Ewen Callaway, "Using Tetris to Heal Trauma," *New Scientist*, January 7, 2009. www.newscientist.com/blogs/shortsharpscience.html.

David Dobbs, "The Costs of War: A Study Reignites the Debate over Soldiers' Trauma," *Scientific American*, January 30, 2007. www.sciam.com/blog/60-second-science.cfm.

Kimberly Dozier, "Reporters Notebook: The War over PTSD," *CBS Evening News*, December 20, 2007. www.cbsnews.com/stories/2007/12/20/notebook/main3637137.shtml.

A. Chris Gajilan, "Iraq Vets and Post-Traumatic Stress: No Easy Answers, CNN, October 24, 2008. www.cnn.com/2008/HEALTH/conditions/10/24/ptsd.struggle.index.html.

Amanda Gardner, "9/11's Psychological Scars Healing Slowly," *U.S. News & World Report*, September 11, 2008. www.usnews.com.

Heidi Harrom, "Secondary Prevention of Posttraumatic Stress Disorder with Propranolol," 2007. http://psychiatry.mc.duke.edu.

Debra Kaufman, "Virtual Iraq: A VR Solution Helps Combat Post-Traumatic Stress Disorder," *Computer Graphics World*, August 2008. *General Reference Center Gold*. Gale. Public Trial Site, August 26, 2008. www.cgw.com/Publications/CGW/2008/Volume-31-Issue-8-Aug-2008-/Virtual-Iraq.aspx.

Michael D. Lemonick, "War Head Injuries: Long-Term Effects," *Time*, January 31, 2008. www.time.com/time/health/article/0,8599,1708624,00.html.

Debbie Lovell-Hawker, "The Debriefing Debate: Does It Help or Harm?" InterHealth.org, 2006. www.interhealth.org.uk.

Christie Nicholson, "Surviving a Plane Crash," *Scientific American*, January 20, 2009. www.sciam.com/podcast/episode.cfm?id=surviving-a-plane-crash-09-01-20.

Elisabeth Salemme, "Vietnam Vets: Helping Iraq War Trauma," *Time*, June 11, 2008. www.time.com/time/nation/article/0,8599,1813593,00.html.

Sally Satel, "The Trouble with Traumatology," *Weekly Standard*, February 19, 2007. www.aei.org/publications/pubID.25600.

Nikhil Swaminathan, "Fuggedaboudit, or Remember—It Just Takes Practice," *Scientific American*, July 12, 2007. www.sciam.com/article.cfm?id=suppressing-memories-takes-practice.

Claudia Wallis, "Genes and Post-Traumatic Stress," *Time*, March 18, 2008. www.time.com/time/health/article/0,8599,172304,00.html.

INDEX

A

Adler-Nevo, Gili, 40

Adults, 46–53

Akerib, Vivian, 72

Allen, Scott, 66

American Journal of Bioethics, 88

Americans with Disabilities Act (1990), 119

Amygdala, *90*

Anger, 58

Anti-Defamation League, 130

Associated Press, 60, 89

B

Barlow, David, *69,* 69–70

Biological Psychiatry (journal), 86

Birmes, Philippe, 72

Black, James W., 94

Bodkin, J. Alexander, 67, 71

Bower, H., 132

Bower, Karen, 118–119

Bradley, Rebekah, 64

Brain

of children, 61

fear/stress and, *64*

lesions, 32

memory formation and, 92

propranolol and, 86

Brief psychodynamic psychotherapy, 51

Brunet, Alain, 72, 91, 92, 93

C

Cahill, Larry, 91–92

Chemtob, Claude, 41

Child-centered therapy (CCT), 39

Childhood abuse/trauma, 10, 63–64

Children

diagnosis of PTSD in, 76–77

as Holocaust survivors, 135–137

PTSD in, 17, 20, 36–45

traumatic events and, 10–11, 12

Clinical Child Psychology and Psychiatry (journal), 39, 41

Cognitive behavioral therapy (CBT), 22

in adults, 47

in children, 37–40

Coleman, Penny, 24, 105

Columbine High School shooting (1999), 9, *11,* 12, 117

Combat trauma, 54–59

Coping techniques, 55

Cox, Sandra, 114, 118